Behavior Sampler

Behavior Sampler

by Gary Wilkes

Published by C&T Publishing
Second Printing
Book design by Tri Star Printing and Visual Communications

ISBN: 1-889854-03-4
Formerely ISBN: 0-9624017-2-2
Library of Congress Catalog Card Number: 94-69125

Foreword

by Connie Jankowski, Editor, DOGS ★U★S★A★

I talk to my dog. Misha understands me. We don't discuss politics or how to decorate the family room, but we converse. Some of our conversations are simple. She understands "Let's go upstairs," and "Are you hungry?" She responds to about one hundred cues. She happily heels, retrieves and sneezes on command.

But many of our conversations are nonverbal. She waits at the door until I get out my keys. She can tell when I need a hug and when I'm too tired to jog around the block. A glance to the right or left can be her signal to head in that direction. We communicate in many ways. Her head on my knee tells me she's content. My quick movements tell her I'm stressed.

Misha and I have developed an understanding. We live in harmony without getting in each other's way. How have we come to this point? After 14 years of living together we've had a lot of practice communicating; however, without understanding canine behavior and without undertaking formal training classes we might not have progressed to this point.

Pets are wonderful. We've heard it, we believe it, but is it really true?

Dogs serve man in many ways. They work the fields, they assist the physically challenged and they provide emotional support to their owners. However, many dogs do not follow the pattern; instead they add stress to their owners' lives. Some dogs are cherished and others are nuisances. What makes the difference?

No one acquires a dog with the intention of creating a monster. Whether puppy or senior citizen, dogs are chosen by their owners to mirror images learned from examples of dogs they have known or those seen in media. Frustrations mount when owners realize that their dogs aren't Lassies, and that the neighbor must have a secret that enabled his dog to become so endearing.

How can one ensure that his or her dog will meet expectations? Will an obedience class solve problems with dogs? Do veterinarians have the answers? Are dogs genetically programmed to be good or bad? Will feeding premium dog food make a dog bigger, stronger or smarter? While looking for simple, cure-all answers to difficult questions, many pet owners fail to realize that owning a pet is a serious commitment, which requires investment of time to achieve the goal of developing a well-adjusted, enjoyable pet.

Whether a dog is acquired to be a pet, a show dog or a working dog, the same rules apply for achieving your goal. Choose wisely. Train and condition. Provide solid health care and keep your dog groomed. Consider the whole dog. A flea-ridden, worm-infested dog will not be able to concentrate on holding a sit-stay. A poorly socialized dog will stress out on visits to the veterinarian. An aggressive dog cannot be groomed. The whole dog is the sum of its parts. Dog training is not limited to the 15-minutes-a-day you schedule to practice heeling and stays. Learning takes place every minute of the day. Provide your dog with a healthy environment, and it will flourish.

Birds gotta fly, fish gotta swim . . . and so the old song goes. Animal behavior is a fascinating subject, and understanding why your dog acts as it does can help you live in harmony. Allow your dog to be a dog. Set rules, stick by them, but be sure your expectations are realistic. Enrolling in a dog-training class can be the best decision you make regarding your dog—or it can be the worst. The advice your receive and the instructions you follow will shape your relationship with your dog.

Not all dog owners find this harmony. The Massachusetts Society for the Prevention of Cruelty to Animals plays an info-recording for callers placed on hold. They cite an overwhelming statistic on this recording: More dogs die each year because of behavior problems than from all diseases combined. How many of these dogs could have been saved with proper training?

In this book, author Gary Wilkes shares his experiences and his feelings about dogs he has known. His insights and reflections will help you to understand the whole dog. Wilkes takes a no-nonsense look at dogs in society. He complements that with sound behavioral theories that awaken the reader to a new approach to training.

Are these theories off-the-wall and experimental? No, the basis of Wilkes' recommendations can be recognized in the works of noted behaviorists who have coined such "household phrases" as behavior modification and classical conditioning. Anyone who has passed Psych 80 at any university will consider this leisure reading. Beware the trainer who has jumped on the "behavioral bandwagon" without adequate preparation. While understanding canine behavior is key to understanding man's best friend, concepts can be misunderstood and damaging, as Wilkes points out. Rarely have these concepts been presented as accurately and concisely as in this book.

Although academically based, anyone can comprehend the text. After reading this book you will be prepared to evaluate trainers, books and videos, sorting the sound from the simply slick.

Wilkes recognizes the whole dog; you will enjoy his anecdotes and illustrations. Reading his book will provide you with insight necessary to understand your dog and develop a communication system. If you care enough to acquire this book and read through it you and your dog will reap untold benefits. You are likely to join the ranks of the success stories of responsible pet ownership. You will experience the human/animal bond. You will know the magic of having a canine companion, in the deepest extent of the phrase. Your life will be enriched beyond imagination; you will have a Misha.

Introduction

In the mid 1970's, I began working for a small humane society in Oregon. I had little experience with animals and even less experience with the realities of pet overpopulation. The Executive Director, Doug Fakkema, told me something that gave me hope. According to Doug, my lack of animal savvy was not a liability — animal skills could be learned. After almost 20 years, I can assure you; he was right.

This collection of articles reflects what I have learned about animals and my search for humane ways to change their behavior. Rather than focusing on the misbehavior of animals, I have tried to include a broader spectrum of topics, from learning theory to humane issues. With the exception of the article entitled "A First Look at House-training," (one of my Dog Fancy columns) these articles ran in the Tribune and on the Cox and New York Times Wire services. The narrative articles are primarily composites of true events that do not reflect any particular person or animal. The animals mentioned in "Lifestyles of the Weird and Wacky" are all real animals whom I have witnessed performing their unique behaviors.

One of the pleasures of my job has been the diversity of people and animals that I have had the opportunity to work with. I hope this collection will mirror that variety and offer you a true sampling of what animals do. Enjoy!

Acknowledgments

This collection of articles represents two aspects of my life; my knowledge of animals and the practice of writing about it. For the first part, I would like to thank Doug Fakkema, who started and shaped my years in the humane movement—Dean Bauman, DVM, for letting me tag along. I would like to thank Peter Killeen, Ph.D. for teaching me about the science of operant conditioning.

For the second part, writing about animals, I am deeply grateful to Cox Publishing, Jeff Bruce and Liz Merrit for their support of my Tribune newspaper column.

To my editing team, Sandy Duxbury and my wife Michele, I am eternally grateful for several million hours of their valuable time, and the fact that they have refrained from murdering me, so far.

I would like to extend special thanks to the veterinarians, staff, clients and their pets who have allowed me to practice a profession that I truly love.

To my wife Michele

Contents

Chapter 1: Modern Training

Chapter 2: Problem Behavior

Chapter 3: Cats, Cats, Cats

Chapter 4: Care and Keeping

Chapter 5: Acquiring a Pet

Chapter 6: The Fruits of Our Labors

Part 1:
Modern Training

Canum Mondo Bizzaro:
Lifestyles of the weird and wacky

In 1970, as a freshman at Oregon State University, I knew a student named Jim Kirby. Jim was an avid bird hunter and had a big Irish Setter named Wooglin. Besides being a reasonably well-trained gun dog, Wooglin had another talent—he could fetch Jim's keys.

In the two-story house that we lived in, Jim could be relaxing on a couch downstairs and simply say "Keys, Wooglin, keys!"

With a bounding leap, the setter would mount the stairs, four at a time, while we waited for the mayhem that invariably ensued. Faint rummaging sounds would come from Jim's room as Wooglin checked out the desk, the floor and any blue jeans that might be lying around. In a few minutes, Wooglin would fly back downstairs with a great flourish, key ring in his mouth, tail wagging and generally pleased with himself.

Many pet owners take great pride in their pets' behavior. From simple but practical acts such as fetching a key ring to more fanciful behaviors, dogs readily adapt in response to reinforcement. While having a dog perform a unique behavior can be a source of pride and accomplishment, it can also have its drawbacks.

Cuervo, a Bull Terrier, was taught to sleep near the baby's room and report to her owners if the child cried in the night. Her way of alerting her owners was to launch her compact 40 pound frame in a high arc and drop like a rock between their sleeping forms. The behavior eventually disappeared as the baby started sleeping through the night, much to the owner's relief.

Dozer, a Rottweiler mix, loved to fling his toys around the house. In order to limit the mess, he was taught to put them back into a basket, on command. This satisfied everyone until the day that Dozer's owner lost his wallet. After two days of frantic searching, the proverbial "last place" was searched—Dozer's basket held the missing wallet.

Even the ritual of fetching the newspaper is not immune to animal creativity. One client of mine groggily let his dog out to fetch the paper one morning and then forgot to let the dog back in. When he realized his mistake, he opened his front door and found Fido dutifully sitting amid a pile of about a dozen of his neighbors' newspapers.

Perhaps the strangest learned behavior I have seen was performed by a standard Dachshund. His owner had a small fish tank that she regularly cleaned. Her routine included placing a smaller fish bowl next to the tank, to temporarily hold the fish while she cleaned their tank. The dog had learned to pluck the fish from the tank, gently with his mouth, and place them unharmed in the bowl. The owner could then clean the tank and change the water. When the owner commanded "Put them back, now," the dog placed the fish back in the tank again, apparently no worse for wear.

For most pet owners, these types of behaviors are hard to imagine. Conjuring up an interesting behavior is one thing, actually teaching the animal to do it is another. Since behaviors of this type are so rare, it is easy to assume that the animal simply taught itself. A more realistic view would look for specific ways that the behaviors were encouraged.

Wooglin's fetching behavior was a modification of his skill at retrieving. Cuervo's reaction to a crying baby was taught by playing a tape recording of the baby crying and then asking the dog to "come." Dozer's behavior of playing wildly with his toys also included taking a toy to his owner and dropping it on the ground.

His owners then added a basket to the routine. When Dozer approached them with a toy, they set a basket under his mouth and asked him to drop it. By reinforcing his behavior only when he hit the target, they quickly taught Dozer the behavior.

As for the fishing Dachshund—like all good fishermen, he asked me not to reveal his secrets.

How hot dogs can make "Hot Dogs"

Some dog trainers refuse to use food in training. Their rationale is that a dog should be expected to work out of loyalty and that using food will cause the animal to always expect treats in exchange for a performance. This distorted view of training fails to acknowledge the most effective trainer of all—nature.

Long before Lassie or Rin Tin Tin, wild dogs and wolves hunted for food. Canadian wolves, for instance, attack ten caribou for every one they kill. Because they are never assured that they will be successful, they always work as hard as they can. It is not food that makes an animal get lazy or work poorly, it is something far more devastating—a sure thing.

In contrast to his wild cousins, Rover has a pretty soft life. Besides a constantly filled bowl of premium dog food, he is on permanent vacation. His day is filled with snoozing and watching the birds go by. His owner is in a loving but predictable rut. Every night at ten o'clock, Rover gets his num-nums. His owner begs Rover to sit, lie down, roll over and speak. Rover just stands there. Eventually he gets his Milkbone in exchange for outwaiting his owner—not much of a behavior.

After several months of this, you can forget about Rover performing for a Milkbone at all. He knows that if he holds out long enough he's going to get it anyway. Even if he misses a Milkbone, he always has food in his bowl. Rover taught his owner that trick long ago, by banging his metal food bowl around after midnight.

If Rover's owner wants to correct this problem he can learn how to use food effectively. An excerpt from Rover's diary might give us a clue about the procedure.

7:00 AM—Up as usual for my morning snack while my master gets ready for work. I trotted down to the old food bowl and just about died. It was empty. I picked it up and banged it against the tile. That usually works if I just keep banging it around. My master dutifully came to fill my bowl. I couldn't believe my eyes. He didn't fill the bowl. He put it on the counter! Then he left!

4:00 PM—I am starving to death. If I hadn't stashed that rawhide bone behind the couch I'd be dead, for sure.

6:00 PM—My master finally came home and just fed the cat. I can't wait until he fills my bowl. I danced and sat and rolled over and barked for at least two minutes, but he just walked away from me. I can't stand this!

7:00 PM—I walked up to my master a moment ago wagging my tail furiously. He barked something at me. I vaguely remember the sound from puppy class, years ago. I think it was "SIT." I rolled over and barked. He had the gall to walk away from me again. What does it take to satisfy this guy?

8:00 PM—Finally I got my first real morsel of food today. He said "SIT" again and so I tried sitting down. He said some other words to me and gave me a biscuit. I have never had a better tasting biscuit in my life. He walked a few feet away and asked me to sit again. I did, but this time he only patted me on my head. I guessed, correctly, that he didn't like the style of my sitting, so on the next attempt I dropped my bottom so fast I felt the floor sag. We must have done it 30 or 40 times. He is suddenly very picky about how I sit. Sometimes he didn't give me anything at all; he just walked away. I was so hungry I really didn't care as long as I could figure out some way to get the food.

10:00 PM—I finally got my dinner. He asked me to "SIT" again, so I tried to stand very still until he gave it to me. He spun around and shut the bedroom door in my face for fifteen minutes! He asked me again finally and I hope I don't have to tell you that I sat faster than a rabbit at a greyhound convention. Diary, I am hoping that my master's insanity is only temporary. It may be a long process to cure him. Just when I thought I had him perfectly trained . . .

Superstitious behaviors

Many people are cautious about letting a black cat walk across their path. I know a black cat who is absolutely terrified of anyone who bakes cookies. Sam is a superstitious cat.

About 60 years ago, the behaviorist, B.F. "Fred" Skinner, invented an interesting machine. It was a complex box that could provide a variety of conditions to test how animals learn. The major advantage of a "Skinner box" was that the animal was allowed to participate in the experiment without the interference of the human experimenter. A simple setup included a colored light and a typewriter key. If the pigeon pecked the key while the light was on, a mechanism could both count the peck and drop some corn into a hopper. By adapting to the box, the pigeon could figure out what "caused" the corn. The pigeon's behavior would change in order to get the corn. The ability to count how often the pigeon pecked, and the rate at which corn was delivered was a scientific breakthrough.

Soon after Skinner started using his box, he discovered something remarkable. He set the mechanism to dump corn into the hopper at random times. There was no connection between the appearance of the corn and any particular behavior that the pigeon might perform. The pigeon could do anything, or nothing and still get fed—at random times. The pigeon amazed the researchers by developing new behaviors anyway.

To appreciate this, it is necessary to imagine the pigeon's view of the process. Gertrude, the pigeon, is moving slowly around the box. She hears the sound of corn falling into the hopper. She gobbles greedily but is still hungry. Gertrude may now ask herself, "What caused the corn, and can I make it happen again?" You and I know that her quest is hopeless. Gertrude knows something we don't, however. Just before the corn fell into the hopper, Gertrude had turned to her left. After eating, she turned to her left again. Within a few seconds the corn fell into the hopper again. Gertrude was now convinced that if she just kept turning to the left she would receive a treat. She was absolutely right. Because the box is set up to reinforce her randomly, any behavior that she selects will eventually lead to more corn. Even though her behavior has nothing to do with when and how she gets corn, she will end up performing useless behaviors over and over again.

About a year ago, Sam's owner was baking some cookies. Naturally curious, Sam decided to investigate. As he approached the kitchen, his owner was sliding a hot batch of cookies from the oven. As she lifted the hot cookie sheet, her pot-holder slipped. The hot metal burned her hand. The sheet of cookies flew from her hand and clattered loudly against the counter and then onto the floor. Sam cleared out and hid in the bedroom. Whatever made the loud noise did not follow Sam under the bed. Sam learned his lesson well. If he smells cookies he knows that the cookie monster is loose in the house. The only safe place to be is under the bed. Even though the connection between cookies and flying cookie sheets was accidental, Sam isn't taking any chances.

Many people know of an animal that is displaying superstitious behavior. Dogs that are afraid of new things in their environment often fall into this category. The instinctive fear reaction to anything new can develop a permanent aversion to a part of the yard, or to something as harmless as a spare tire. If a loud noise occurs at the instant that Rover is investigating the tire, he may develop a fear of all tires, or the spot in the yard where the tire lies. Even removing the tire may not change this attitude. To Rover, tires are unlucky.

Ken and Melrene Wasserman, of Everett, Washington, own a Labrador Retriever named Jayboo. Whenever someone laughs, Jayboo spins in circles, as fast as he can. Ken did not set out to teach him the behavior. It happened the same way Gertrude learned to turn left. The first time Jayboo spun, it was to bite a flea on his tail. He spun so fast that he became dizzy and staggered like a drunk. The behavior was so humorous that Ken and Melrene laughed and patted Jayboo on the head. A few more repetitions and the behavior not only happened more often, but it became connected to the sound of laughter. Friends and neighbors helped to perpetuate the behavior until it became a regular part of Jayboo's repertoire. The apparent mysterious development of the behavior makes it even funnier and keeps people laughing and Jayboo spinning.

As a pet owner you can use this knowledge to your advantage. Creating associations between particular behaviors and some reinforcement can keep a dog out of the trash or teach him to spin three times before getting a treat. In essence, all training relies on an animal's willingness to connect unrelated but reinforced events. If a behavior seems unusual, ask yourself how the pet could have gained some payoff by performing it. Experiment by using affection and treats to shape and select a small tendency in your animal that can turn into an interesting and unique behavior.

When to say "NO!"

About one hundred years ago, Ivan Pavlov, the Russian physiologist, studied how animals learn about the environment. He suggested that if a dog had to wait for the claws of a bear to sink into his flesh before running from the danger, he could never survive. According to many dog trainers, Pavlov was wrong.

The next time you happen to look at a training book, examine the section about giving corrections. A majority of experts will tell you that the word "NO" should occur at the same time you give a correction. Many do not mention the sequence at all. Others tell you to make the correction, and then say "NO."

To make the importance of this abstraction real, imagine that I have a broom, and the nasty habit of sneaking up from behind and whacking you with it. If you could require me to say the word "duck," would you want me to say it before I hit you, as I hit you, or after I hit you? If you decide to have me yell "duck" before I hit you, you have made the right choice. Any other combination gets you whacked. The answer is simple—the signal must come before the correction. Since this answer seems absurdly obvious, you might wonder why all those experts haven't figured it out yet. The answer lies with a topic foreign to many dog trainers—human instinct.

Language and speech are learned behaviors. Until we are about a year old, we do not use language. We instinctively grab and push things long before we learn to ask for them. As adults, when confronted with a new situation, we fall back on our instinctive reactions—we jerk the chain first, and then warn the dog. This is identical to the old saying about closing the barn door after the horses are loose.

All this scientific stuff is well and good, you might say, but what does it mean in the real world? Is it really important to know about broom whacking? How can the timing of my warning change the effect of the whack?

To illustrate the use of this knowledge, let's look at the standard tool of dog training—the choke chain. A choke chain is designed to quickly constrict around a dog's neck. This unpleasant experience is intended to teach the dog not to pull. As the dog walks next to his owner, he is jerked swiftly if he gets out of position. This is the same as the simultaneous broom whacker. The dog has no warning of the jerk. The dog's behavior will change based on the exact instant that the chain was jerked. Only a person who jerks many dogs will be able to apply the correction with perfect timing. The average pet owner will not be effective with this method. Either the owner ends up jerking the chain forever, or the dog winds up strangling himself in a continuous pulling match.

The advice of the professional trainer cannot instantly give a person perfect timing. The hobbyist needs some sort of advantage over the trainer's many hours of experience. An experienced broom whacker can solve this problem instantly. The missing link in traditional training is the absence of a signal that means "duck."

Our broom whacker tells Joe Pet-owner to start saying the word "no" at the instant that Fido gets out of position. Then the pet owner gives the leash correction. Fido is going to be amazed at this new turn of events. As he starts to surge forward, he hears that funny word, "No." Then he gets "whacked" by the choke chain. Over the next series of repetitions, something odd happens. Fido begins to move ahead of Joe, but hesitates and then decides to remain in the correct position. He has changed his behavior based on where he was when Joe Pet-owner said "No." After several repetitions, the advantage is obvious. Joe Pet-owner does not have to jerk the chain with perfect timing. He merely has to say "no" on time. This word allows him to deliver the actual correction a couple of seconds later and still duplicate the professional trainer's timing.

Science is often seen as a cold and distant subject of little use in the real world. Pavlov's simple analogy about the dog and the bear was derived from scientific observation. It eloquently contradicts common knowledge and practice. Using techniques firmly rooted in science can make a dramatic difference in your pet's behavior. The fact that a method is traditional does not insure that it is effective. So, the next time someone tells you to say "no" at the same time you correct your dog—tell him to duck, instead.

Shamu's school for whales

If you visit a major marine park you will probably be dazzled by the intricate and spectacular routines of dolphins and whales. Have you ever imagined what it would be like if you were their trainer? Where would you start? If you want to find out, grab a bucket of fish and follow me.

First you need to realize that learning is often hard work. Before you can teach a behavior you must find something your dolphin is willing to work for—like fish. Armed with a bucket of fish you must now select a behavior. Hmmmmm. Flipper doesn't speak English. You can't just ask him to do something. As you sit pondering your problem, the dolphin leaps in a graceful arc to get a better look at you. Aha! That's a behavior isn't it? You are so overjoyed you toss a mackerel to your new friend. He swims to the fish and gobbles it greedily. Your excitement drops as you realize that you still don't know what to do.

About fifteen minutes later your dolphin leaps again. As he lands in the water you toss another fish. You repeat this performance each time he jumps. At the end of your first day he has jumped ten times. On day two, you keep up the pace and Flipper jumps 15 times. On the third day you are amazed to find that he jumps a whopping 20 times. The increase in the tendency that this dolphin will jump from the water is caused by positive reinforcement. To reinforce means to strengthen, so you have reinforced, or strengthened the behavior.

Now that Flipper is jumping 20 times per day, how do you get him to jump higher? If you throw a fish to him in mid-air you will distract him and ruin the jump. You could start giving him extra fish for higher jumps but it would take forever to get the point across. You need to be able to tell him exactly what you liked about the jump, instantly. Now you know why the other trainers wear those water-proof whistles.

Before you can teach an animal accurate behaviors, you must first teach the equivalent of the word "yes." Dolphin trainers start by blowing a whistle and then giving the animal a fish. This process is repeated until the dolphin visibly startles when it hears the whistle. To the dolphin, the whistle means that a fish is on the way. The sound, followed by the fish, strengthens any behavior that the dolphin was doing when the whistle blew. The whistle bridges the gap from the instant the animal does something correctly until the time it takes for him to get his fish. Now you can shape behaviors with an accuracy impossible to someone who merely tosses fish around.

Now that your dolphin is jumping consistently, it is time to select a cue that can get Flipper to jump on command. First thing in the morning you let him into the training tank. Because you have worked exclusively on jumping, you know that he will perform that particular behavior. As he rushes into the tank, he hears a new noise. You have set up a speaker and you are broadcasting a low-pitched continuous sound underwater. As the dolphin starts leaping, you reinforce his leaps with your "whistle and fish." Suddenly you chop off the tone and walk away from the tank. Flipper is decidedly confused and frustrated.

After several days of this routine your dolphin will learn an important piece of information. He can only get fish if he leaps when he hears the special tone. If the dolphin hesitates, shut off the tone and walk away. This insures that he will jump when he hears the sound. Now you are ready for an audience.

The next day, your audience files into the stadium and fills the bleachers. You open the gate and your dolphin charges into the tank, swimming underwater. As the narration introduces Flipper, you step on the button that produces the special tone. With a rush of water, a lean, streamlined creature rockets from the water in a breath-taking leap. You blow your whistle at the instant Flipper hits the top of the jump. You take your foot from the button and your pupil disappears as quickly as he came. The oohs and ahhs of astonished tourists swell across the arena.

This is a very simplistic account of the process of teaching an animal one simple behavior. The next time you are at a marine park and fantasize about swimming with Flipper, tip your hat to the patience, skill and hard work of those who make it all look so easy—and then tell the people sitting next to you how it's done.

When egg gets in your eyes

Recently I was at the San Diego Zoo, watching a "Birds of Prey" animal show. A trained hawk was released from a cage, high over the audience's heads. The planned routine called for the hawk to swoop over the crowd to display his fantastic flight abilities. That is what was supposed to happen, but did not. What happened was that a wild hawk flew over the amphitheater and distracted his captive cousin. The "trained" hawk flew off and perched in a tree and refused to return to his handler. The lesson to learn from this experience is that when you are working with animals, don't expect perfection.

There is a tendency on the part of humans to assume that animals are capable of behavioral perfection. We rarely imagine a majestic cougar misjudging a leap and landing on a cactus rather than a deer, but it can happen. Wildlife movies and films tend to reinforce an image of infallible animals until we incorrectly assume that all animals have the ability to do what they want, when they want, flawlessly.

Far from being perfectly robotic, animals survive in an environment that abhors consistency. If all zebras automatically turned left when chased by lions, the lions would be ecstatic—unless all lions automatically turned right when attacking zebras. These absurd examples display an obvious fact; nature requires animals to vary their behavior. The human goal of repetitive, identical behaviors, such as in dog obedience competitions, is actually unnatural and generally unattainable. Expecting a dog to perform the same twelve behaviors in the same order with the same level of enthusiasm in exchange for the same reinforcements is unrealistic. If the same goals were applied to professional baseball, we would expect all players to bat .500, all pitchers would win 50% of their games and spectators would flock to watch more exciting games, such as televised golf.

Obedience competitors are not the only ones with unrealistic expectations of dog perfection. Many owners are startled that their wonderfully trained, six-year old Schnauzer suddenly fails to come when called. The owner's refrain of "He's never done that before," implies the belief that Fritzi's behavior is unchanging and unchangeable. Taking a dog's good behavior for granted is the quickest way to ruin it. Behaviors that are never reinforced often decay and fall apart. Assuming that Fritzi will always come simply because he has always done so is risky thinking. A better approach would be to give Fritzi a treat every once in a while, for correct behavior.

Another feature of this belief in behavioral perfection, is the idea that an animal may be a "perfect failure." This assumption of perfect failure may be an artificial limitation on a dog's learning potential. If Rover has jumped on some guests, it does not mean that he will jump on all guests, or that he cannot learn to sit instead of jump. For the owner, it is easiest to assume Rover would jump on all guests. The perfectionist's solution is to confine Rover when guests arrive, rather than teach him correct behavior. A more realistic approach recognizes that Rover is capable of varying his behavior and therefore is capable of improving his method for greeting guests. Replacing the jumping with an acceptable behavior may solve the greater problem. Allowing Rover to be "less than perfect" during his initial training and gradually increasing his level of competence will usually solve the problem quickly.

Expecting a dog to walk perfectly at heel, at all times, is another example of pet perfectionism. Most dogs are supremely challenged when expected to ignore every new sight and smell that they come in contact with. Wise owners limit the enforced heeling aspects of a walk and allow for periods of loose-leash sniffing and sight-seeing. Periodically expecting perfection for a limited period of time is a much more realistic goal for your pet.

One of the pleasures of owning a pet is the animal's ability to offer unique and interesting behavior. Allowing animals to be themselves includes occasionally letting them behave erratically.

Demanding robot-like performance or assuming that any mistakes are signs of spite or malice denies their basic nature. When living with pets it is important to accept their mistakes as a part of their total personality and to remember, "they're only non-human."

What's in a name?

I was in the market the other day when I saw a little book of potential names for new babies. Inside were over 1000 names and their meanings, with things like—Peter comes from a Greek word that means "rock" and Winifred is Old English for "washed ashore after a squall." While humans can obviously understand names that describe personal attributes or conditions, have you ever wondered what your animals might imagine their names mean? Here's a simple multiple choice question that can help you find out.

1) Your pet should think its name means . . .
   a) absolutely nothing
   b) come
   c) NO!
   d) stop, look, wait for the next command.

The correct answer for this test is "d"—which is also the least likely to be true.

One reason for this paradox is that while humans think of a name in terms of identity, animals respond to names as signals associated with certain behaviors. A human names a Schnauzer "Blitz" to describe the Germanic heritage of his breed type, while Blitz thinks his name means "Run away, before the two-legged giant whacks you with a newspaper."

The reason for this discrepancy is simple—Blitz has inadvertently learned that his name actually means "No!" For instance, when Blitz moves to raid the trash, his owner is far more likely to yell "Blitz!" rather than a simple "no!" If his owner consistently uses his name and then scolds or punishes him, an association between the sound "Blitz" and scolding is inevitable. Soon the dog will flinch and run when he hears his name.

Some owners go even farther in teaching this association. The most common variation on this theme is to yell the dog's name and then scream NO! ("Blitz, NO!") Supposedly, this practice allows you to punish one dog while sparing another. The reasoning is that if Witchy, the Wheaten Terrier, is minding her own business, yelling "Blitz, No!" will effect him but not her. While this may be logical for humans, a closer look shows that it is confusing for dogs.

First, if Witchy knows her name correctly, she is not going to be listening when you call "Blitz." The first thing she is going to hear is the word "NO!" screamed at her. Though she may be perfectly innocent of any offense, she will assume she is being punished for whatever she is doing when she hears the word "NO!"

From Blitz's view, the scene is equally confusing. Just as he picks up a bedroom slipper, he hears his master call his name. He drops the slipper and responds promptly by turning to face his master—that's when he hears the word "NO!" Instead of thinking that picking up the slipper was the bad behavior, Blitz is now convinced that looking at his owner was the evil act. The dogs have each learned different lessons from this experience. From now on, Witchy may become generally leery of her owner, and Blitz will start purposely avoiding his name.

Another common misuse of a dog's name is when it ultimately means "come," rather than "attention." The easiest way to teach this, is to yell the dog's name when you want to discover his location. If Fido is out of sight, the easiest way to find him is to call the dog's name. As he shows up to investigate your call, it is natural for you to praise him for coming. A few weeks of enthusiastic greetings and the dog has figured out that his name means "come and get it."

While many owners do not see the harm in using an animal's name in place of the word "come," the practice hides a dangerous possibility. If Fido runs out the front door and across the street, you may have a serious problem. If there are cars whizzing by, you must have a way to warn Fido and tell him to stay. The problem is that he thinks "Fido" means "come." In this scenario, you cannot get his attention without also triggering the command to "come"—which may cause an accident.

For those of you who answered that a dog's name means "absolutely nothing," you have astute powers of observation—many animals do not react to their names at all. One reason for this is the common practice of constantly, and inappropriately, using the dog's name. "Fifi, sit!, Fifi, come, Fifi, this, Fifi, that, Fifi, Fifi, FIFI!" The owner simply tacks the name onto everything, but never waits to see if the dog responded correctly. Soon the name has less and less meaning for the dog.

Teaching your pet to stop, look and listen is an important behavior. It allows you to control your pet from a distance and insure that he will focus on you in an emergency. Regardless of the fancy-sounding name you pick for your pet, make sure your pet knows what it really means—stop, look and listen!

The Dinah's Effect:
The variable makes Rover very able.

At the age of fifteen, I got my first job. I worked as a busboy at Dinah's Chicken and Pancake house for $1.15 per hour. After a few months of hard work, I discovered what is meant by the phrase "to work like a dog." No matter how hard I worked, I always got the same reward. I also learned something that dogs seem to know instinctively—if you are paid the same no matter how hard you work, you will eventually do the least amount of work necessary to get the paycheck. I call this the "Dinah's Effect."

In the initial stages of teaching an animal to do something, it is necessary to consistently reinforce correct behavior. Scientists call this a fixed rate of reinforcement—one sit earns one treat. Besides acting to strengthen a response, each reinforcement also provides a piece of the puzzle and gives the animal information about which behavior is being reinforced. To put it simply, the animal sits because sitting seems to bring treats and praise.

Once the animal understands what is expected, however, a fixed rate of reinforcement quickly leads to the dreaded "Dinah's Effect." When Rover discovers that extra effort will not bring extra reinforcements, he will sit only if he knows that you have a biscuit, and only if he's hungry. Soon his response will be lackluster and indifferent. Contrary to popular belief, this problem is not the result of using food as a reinforcer, but with the rate at which it was given. The solution to this problem is relatively simple—Rover needs to switch from a fixed rate of reinforcement to a more variable one.

Scientific research and common sense tell us that variable reinforcement is far stronger than fixed rates. The widespread appeal of slot machines, carnival midway games and most forms of gambling is due to this principle. The allure of great wealth in exchange for a nominal risk is hard to resist. To test this, all we have to do is convince Rover that instead of his normal obedience routine, he is actually playing the new canine carnival game, "Sit Quickly."

The rules to "Sit Quickly" are simple. Rover gets to try his skill at sitting in order to win treats. His task is simply to respond to your command—instantly. If he does, he gets ten times his normal reward. If he hesitates or sits for only a moment, he loses and has to try again.

At first, Rover is going to be frustrated with this change in the rules. In the past, he has always won the prize easily. Suddenly his success is not assured, and neither is his treat. He will be tempted to quit. To prevent this, you must make sure that he gets a substantial jackpot early in the game. If he believes that his goal is achievable and that it could pay off with a jackpot, he will persevere through his mistakes.

Once Rover is convinced that the grand prize is just around the corner, he will start offering the behavior enthusiastically, but not necessarily expertly. Some of these responses will necessarily be better than others. Since sitting "quickly" is a subjective standard, you will have trouble at first deciding when to give him jackpots and when to withhold reinforcement. Your best guideline is to give Rover "extras for excellence." Whenever he improves, give him more than usual. As his standard of performance rises, the jackpots will automatically become fewer and farther between as it becomes harder for him to top his own best performance.

As Rover's performance starts to become consistently better, raise your standards again. Now you can demand two or three perfect tries before you even give verbal praise. Dole out your rewards sparingly for mediocre attempts and lavishly for exceptional performance. Soon Rover's overall ability to sit quickly will be enhanced. His attitude about training in general will also improve dramatically.

Assuming that a dog will work "like a dog" for meager and consistent rewards is an unrealistic expectation. Learning to vary the reinforcements according to the animal's level of performance will create better behavior while removing the constant need for food rewards. Better yet, avoiding the Dinah's Effect by giving bonuses for great behavior may give you a bonus too—a truly happy dog.

How to get your dog into Carnegie Hall

There is an old joke about a visitor to New York City who asks a local how to get to Carnegie Hall. The New Yorker's wry answer is "Practice, practice, practice."

Most people understand that to become skillful at anything, one must practice. This is assumed to be true for behaviors such as playing the violin, flying an airplane or performing brain surgery. It is ironic that this belief stops short when we consider our pets.

For instance, Cliff has a St. Bernard named Mortimer, who embarrasses him whenever guests come to the house. At the first sound of the doorbell, Mort bellows like a bull and charges the door. When Cliff opens the door, he holds Mort by the collar while the guest tries to slip past. When the guest finally sits down, Mortimer shoves his face in the lap of his newest friend.

In case you don't know, most St. Bernards carry a load of drool in their mouths at all times. Mortimer is no exception. Mortimer's victim now has several large strings of slime smeared across his legs. Mortimer is not a big hit with Cliff's friends.

Cliff has always tried to get Mortimer to be nice when people come over. He waits on pins and needles as his guests sit on the couch and then begins his apology, as Mort approaches the guest. Just as Mort slimes the person, Cliff yells at the dog and bodily drags him off to his kennel. On the surface it looks as if Mort has failed again—but a closer look shows that the problem is elsewhere.

Cliff has forgotten that learning requires repetitions. Each time a guest comes over, Mortimer gets only one chance to succeed or fail. Sometimes it is as much as a week between visitors. The few successful repetitions are so far apart that Mortimer forgets what he has learned from week to week.

To help Mort through this dilemma, Cliff must restructure the situation to allow for many repetitions in a short amount of time. The following is an example of a typical training session.

The doorbell rings—Mortimer races to the door. Cliff tells Mort that he is wasting his time. No one is coming into the house until Mort sits. Mort barks for a few seconds and then realizes that Cliff isn't going to answer the door. Cliff's accomplice waits until Mortimer is quiet and then rings the doorbell again. The process is repeated until the sound of the doorbell fails to elicit a response from Mort.

After Mort's initial reaction is extinguished, it is time to get a little tougher. This time, as the bell rings, Cliff stands and walks toward the door. Mort returns instantly to his old behavior—as if it had never been extinguished. As Mort starts to go wild, Cliff says "Wrong" in a normal tone of voice and sits back down. The "doorbell" person waits until Mort shuts up.

Each time Mort breaks and rushes to the door, Cliff says "Wrong." Soon even the entrance of the guest does not cause Mort to go crazy. Each failure leads to the word "wrong" and the quick exit of the guest. Mort soon learns that barking, sliming or jumping causes people to leave.

On his first day of training, Mort saw this pattern unfold about 50 times over about 30 minutes. On the first repetition, Mort gave his typical wild reaction. By the time he had heard the bell ring for the 50th time, he did not charge the front door, jump on the guest or slime the person's lap. Cliff had taught him the first step toward politeness without lifting a finger.

Later that afternoon, Cliff's friend comes for a second round of training. Mort acts like an idiot for the first three repetitions and then settles down—much faster than usual. On the fourth repetition, Mort is perfectly behaved. Cliff praises him and gives him a big doggie treat for a great performance.

After several training sessions, Mort became quite consistent in his correct response to the door. Without resorting to harsh treatment, Cliff had changed Mort's behavior through consistent reinforcement over many repetitions.

Cliff is so pleased with Mort's behavior he's thinking of getting him into show-biz—now that he knows how to get to Carnegie Hall.

Dogs are not mimics—exactly

John owns a 4-year-old Retriever named Murphy. He adopts a second dog named Houdini. A former owner had great fun teaching Houdini to open gate latches with his nose. After several escapes, John gives Houdini back to his original owner. Will Murphy now know how to escape by nudging the latch with his nose? Give yourself ten points if your answer was no. Dogs are not "copy cats."

True mimicry is the ability to consciously imitate the behavior of another. Horses, cats, apes, dolphins and humans all have this ability—dogs do not. Imitation is a powerful survival mechanism that allows one animal to learn from the mistakes and success of another. While dogs do not possess the equivalent of "monkey see, monkey do," they do have a behavior that makes up for it. Dogs have an instinctive tendency to follow each other around.

By being in close proximity, dogs share many experiences. When one dog is attacked by a mountain lion, the whole pack will respond and share in the experience. Each dog learns from the encounter, but not by watching his packmates. He learns based on whether or not his behavior saved him from the lion's claws. This creates as many different responses to a situation as there are dogs. Dogs have survived because they can offer many varieties of attack and defense. If they learned from watching each other, they would all perform in one fashion and the group would be far less able to adapt to new situations.

Unless you understand this process, living with a dog can be a frustrating experience. Many pet owners are unaware that they must individually teach certain behaviors to a new dog. They assume that their older dog will instruct the younger. If the behavior requires the younger dog to follow the older dog, learning may take place. Many pups learn to wander through a doggie door by playing follow the leader. The pup will not learn to bark to tell you he must go outside, however. An awareness of your dog's abilities and limitations will help you develop a good relationship with your pet and avoid ulcers. Here are some examples of how to use this information:

- Don't teach your dog to sit by sitting down yourself and putting a milkbone in your mouth. If dogs were capable of true mimicry this would work. This behavior must be taught individually.

- If your dog makes a mess, don't worry about whether the dog sees you clean it up or not. Claims that your dog will continue making messes because he saw you clean it up are wrong. If he is capable of learning in this way, then all you must do is pretend to eat a milkbone after he watches you clean up the mess. Next time he'll want to clean it up himself.

When logic and reinforcement collide

Pretend that you are walking down the street and happen to see a $100 bill stuck to the lid of a trash dumpster. Will you raise the lid and look inside? If you see another bill inside the dumpster, will you stir the garbage with a stick to look for more? If you see a third bill, just beyond your reach, will you crawl inside? Do you think this behavior is the result of logically weighing the benefits versus the consequences?

If you think this situation is an open and shut case of logical thought, think again. Here comes the real question. Would you look in the dumpster the next time you pass by? The answer is that even though there is no logical reason why money would be in the dumpster in the first place, you will probably return to look in the magic dumpster. The lure of $100 bills will probably cause you to do something you normally would not. When logic collides with reinforcement, reinforcement usually wins.

Humans are not the only creatures whose behavior is often controlled by reinforcement, rather than conscious thought. Your pet's behavior often reflects this tendency. Given the choice between standing still or jumping up in the air, the average dog would prefer to stay on the ground. The reason he jumps on you when you get home is that he has been positively reinforced since puppyhood for kissing the faces of humans. Jumping on people is as bizarre for a dog as it is for a human to crawl around in a dumpster looking for money. Notice that dogs do not jump up in the air to greet each other. Though there is no logical way to explain why humans want dogs to leap on them, the dogs continue to leap. The behavior is maintained by the gentle attempts of people to push the dog away—something the dog perceives as a form of physical affection.

An example of how negative reinforcement also overcomes logic is the tendency for cats to avoid dirty litter boxes. Negative reinforcement causes behaviors to happen through avoidance. As the litter box gets dirtier, the cat becomes more likely to eliminate in other locations. The cat cannot understand why the box is not clean, only that it is unacceptable. No matter how much the cat may wish to use litter rather than carpet, the reinforcing effect of the dirty box will control the behavior.

Another example of illogical, but reinforced, behavior revolves around your letter carrier. Each day this uniformed intruder invades your dog's space. As the dreaded creature approaches, the dog barks himself silly to drive the letter carrier away. Guess what? It works! As far as the dog is concerned, the barking "caused" the letter carrier to leave, thereby increasing the likelihood that the dog will bark tomorrow and the next day. The dog may generalize his behavior to police uniforms and meter readers. Even though these people are not threats, the dog's aggression may increase—thoughtlessly.

The reason that these examples are so common is that almost all animals have the ability to learn without needing to "think" about it. While instinctive responses are important for survival, it is reinforcement that allows even instinctive behaviors to be modified.

If you stop touching your dog when it jumps on you and give it treats for sitting, jumping behavior will go away. The dog really does not care which behavior it must perform in order to get your approval. The cat who is avoiding a dirty box would gladly stop eliminating on the carpet in exchange for some clean litter and a few cat treats. The dog who hates uniforms can be swayed from his hatred with dog biscuits and other treats. None of these behaviors are the result of conscious thought on the part of the animal, and all of them will respond well to reinforcement.

It is easy to assume that an animal cannot learn because of mental processes such as hate, spite or habit. Complaining that your dog "knows better" or "knows he did wrong" will not solve the problem since "what he knows" is not as important as "what he does." Modifying a behavior is often simply a matter of changing the consequences in such a way that your pet "thinks nothing of it."

Elephants go from carrot and stick to carrot and click.

Question: Of all careers, which is most likely to get you killed?

Need a hint? It is not the obviously risky professions, such as smoke jumper, secret service agent or paparazzi. The most dangerous job in America is that of elephant keeper.

From Hannibal's war elephants to logging operations in Thailand, humans have controlled these largest of land mammals. Over the millennia, techniques of training and control have changed little. A short, wooden rod with a small hook on one end is the primary tool. The handler uses the hook to pull a leg or the trunk, to get the animal to move in a particular direction, or to signal the animal to turn left or right. Confining the animal is achieved by chaining the animal's feet to the ground. Chaining is still a popular method of controlling captive elephants.

While some elephants adapt readily to this system, others do not. In the past, the primary means of controlling "bad" elephants has been to simply increase the amount of force. One danger with this technique is that the force needed to "impress" an elephant runs dangerously close to hurting or terrifying the animal. While intimidation may work for the short run, the old saying about an elephant's memory seems true—they certainly never seem to forget those who have hurt them. It is so easy for an elephant to "accidentally" crush a human that it is not a good idea to be around one that doesn't like you. Untrustworthy elephants are often left chained almost continuously or simply confined in isolation.

To provide proper health care, even chained, dangerous elephants must occasionally be handled. At the San Diego Zoo, behavior specialist Gary Priest is routinely faced with developing novel and humane ways to control these animals. One of Priest's challenges was a male elephant with a history of serious aggression and desperately in need of having his feet groomed. In captivity, elephants build up calluses on the bottoms of their feet. If the calluses are not periodically removed, the animal is eventually unable to walk.

The bull elephant had not had his feet groomed in almost ten years. The traditional method of removing the calluses requires that a keeper stand underneath the elephant and shave the calluses with a sharp tool. In such a vulnerable position, the animal can kill the keeper at any time, either accidentally or intentionally. This animal would have loved the opportunity to "accidentally" squash one of those little "man-critters." For such an openly dangerous elephant, a new "hands-off" approach was necessary.

First, the keepers built a large, seven ton steel gate at one end of the compound. In the center of the gate a hole was cut out— about the size of an elephant's foot. On the "people side" of the gate, a steel stirrup was constructed. Now all that had to be done was to ask a violent, bull elephant to daintily put his tootsies through a blank wall and let strange little creatures hack away at his feet with knives. That's where Gary Priest and his trainers stepped in.

Using methods originally developed for marine mammals, Priest's first job was to teach the animal a signal that means "Good boy." A small tin cricket, or clicker, was associated with carrots. Every time the elephant did something right, he would hear the click that meant "Soup's on!" and then receive a piece of carrot. By timing the clicks correctly, the trainers gradually shaped the behavior, one step at a time. If the animal failed to get it right, the absence of the click told him that he would not get the carrot.

First the animal got clicks and carrots for simply approaching the gate. If he stood still for a couple of seconds he would get another click and treat. Two seconds was parleyed into ten seconds, and then twenty. Next the trainer snapped the clicker when the animal's left, front foot was off the ground one inch. Soon the inch was six inches, and then two feet in the air. A little to the left and the animal's foot was in the stirrup. The elephant was then taught to place each of his other feet into the hole. Soon the animal would voluntarily walk to the gate and put one foot after another into the mysterious hole. He would hold it there while the keeper trimmed the pads of his feet and groomed the animal's nails.

After their success with his feet, the keepers then taught the elephant to allow them to pull his ear through a slot in the gate. The veins on the back of an elephant's ears are convenient for taking blood. Now they could check his health more closely while getting him periodically groomed. The zoo keepers got an unexpected bonus as well. The animal's temperament changed. The level of aggression dropped dramatically. He seemed to enjoy the daily training sessions and stopped charging the gate.

It is too often assumed that the best means of handling an animal is with force and punishment. Behavior programs like the San Diego Zoo's not only solve the immediate issue of control, but build toward an overall improvement in the animal's life. With elephants, traditional "carrot & stick" methods are best replaced with "carrot & click!"

Teaching a dog to "come"

When dogs complain about their owners, they invariably grumble and growl about training. One of the most common complaints is that their owners never teach them how to "come when called." Instead, humans invariably teach dogs that "come" means "I'm going to yell and scream at you, and possibly bop you, you mangy mutt. If you have any brains, you will run away as fast as you can." This problem is accountable for much of the friction between dogs and people.

In fairness, dogs are quick to point out that their owners do teach them many useful behaviors. Many owners regularly provide trash bags full of smelly old chicken, moldy cheese and decayed hamburgers. These canine delicacies teach a dog wonderful qualities such as persistence and creativity. Other commonly taught behaviors include tugging on leashes, chewing on shoes and jumping on guests.

One reason for this discrepancy, according to the dogs, is that the humans do not appear to possess true language. One time a human says, "Get over here this instant, you mangy mutt," while another time the human says, "I told you to get your butt over here, you idiot!" and then, "You better be here by the time I count to five!" These seemingly unrelated statements have no direct translation for the animal. For the dog, this series of apparently random noises is very confusing. While the dog suspects that humans have the potential to be consistent, few dogs have ever witnessed it.

Another reason that dogs believe humans are incapable of true speech is the human habit of chanting unintelligible sounds. The average dog is introduced to this at an early age. The human chants, "SITSITSIT" while shoving down on the dog's rear end.

Then the human says "DOWNDOWNDOWN!" while pushing the dog to the ground. As soon as the dog starts to see some consistency in this process, the human says "SITDOWN-SITDOWN-SITDOWN." The stunned dog has no idea what this combination can possibly mean. This causes the human to say "BAD-DOG-BAD-DOG-BAD-DOG."

Fixing this problem requires a new approach to teaching. Since "common sense" approaches have limited success, we will borrow our technique from a fairy tale. One of Grimm's fairy tales is about Hansel and Gretel, two children who were abandoned in a forest. They knew they would soon lose their way, so they left a trail of bread crumbs on the ground to mark their trail. Hungry birds followed them and devoured the crumbs. While this method did not work for the lost children, it worked beautifully for the birds.

The first step in the Hansel and Gretel method is to find some small, bite-size treats that your dog will work for. Touch a treat to the dog's nose and then drop it on the ground. As Fido remains to gobble the treat, take two steps backward and say "Come." As Fido finishes his treat, he will hear you say "Come" and then look for more treats. Put another treat on the ground, right in front of you. (Make sure he sees you do it.) Now he will come to get the new treat. As he arrives, say "Good boy" and drop another treat on the ground. As he pauses to gobble the new treat, move quickly away from him and say "Come." Repeat this sequence 20 or 30 times.

For the next step, an assistant can be very helpful. Stand about five feet apart and face each other. Each of you will need a handful of treats. Get Fido's attention and ask him to come. When he gets to you, give him the treat. Then your assistant asks him to come. Fido will turn around and go toward the source of the sound. When he gets to the assistant, the assistant says "Good boy" and gives Fido a treat. Repeat this process many times. Gradually move away from each other to make the behavior more difficult. Try hiding behind walls or furniture to make the game interesting.

As Fido gets more accomplished at responding to your requests, you will find that you can replace the treats with toys, praise and affection. It is a good idea to occasionally give him a big food jackpot as a grand prize for great performance. You can gradually move the behavior outdoors to the back yard, a tennis court or other enclosed, safe area. Remember to use the same command every time, and say it only once. If Fido fails to perform the behavior, drop your standards and return to Hansel and Gretel training.

Training by pushing and tugging is "off-target"

Over the years, Bob Hope has become linked with golf. In movies and on stage, he has often held his arms around a beautiful woman and guided her arms through the motion of swinging a club. I think we can agree that teaching golf was the last thing on his mind.

Bob may not know it, but pushing, tugging or guiding someone through a behavior is called modeling. It is the primary way that people teach animals. If you want Spot to sit, shove down on his rear while tugging his neck upward. If Fifi won't come, put a rope on her and reel her in like a tuna. If you want Bruno to sit parallel with you, nudge him with your foot. While these examples are all too common, they are usually quite inefficient. All animals possess an innate resistance to being pushed, shoved or tugged.

A more flexible system of teaching utilizes an animal's instinctive ability to target and track prey. To see this system at work, toss your pet's favorite toy across the room. Aha! The same dog that cannot follow you while on leash can track the toy perfectly and is suddenly skidding across the kitchen floor at almost 20 miles per hour—with no help from the leash.

Now grab the toy and touch it to Fido's nose. As he tries to bite it, move it back over his forehead. Keep it low enough that he does not try to jump up to get it. He will either back up or sit. Next, try your luck at getting Fido to lie down. Touch the toy to his nose and move it in a straight line to his front paws. As Fido tries to grab the toy, move it slowly along the ground away from him. To follow the toy, he must gradually stretch until he is lying down. If he stands up instead, go back to the sitting position and try again. If he succeeds, give him lots of treats and affection.

Controlling a dog's ability to target can go much farther than just laying down or sitting. Most small dogs learn to dance by trying to target a treat over their head. Targeting is the primary behavior used by herding dogs, retrievers and other working animals.

Gunther Gabel-Williams, master circus trainer, uses targeting with his tigers. He uses a stick equipped with a small nail that holds a bit of meat. When he moves the stick, his tigers follow the bit of meat and then receive a reward for the correct action.

House cats adapt readily to training that uses targeting rather than modeling. Pulling and tugging your cat will merely frustrate both of you. Teaching a cat to sit, lie down or roll over can be easily accomplished through targeting.

While many trainers continue to use the age-old method of modeling, targeting reflects a more natural and efficient way to teach. Besides the challenge and enjoyment of teaching without force, your pet's behavior will soon be right on target too!

Happy pets are very variable

My cockatiel Grimmy likes to repeat sounds. Recently he started picking up the first part of Beethoven's 5th Symphony. He would warble the famous DA-DA-DA—DUH over and over again—then something odd happened. His version changed to DA-DA-DUH-DAAA-DUH. Most training is focused on getting an animal to repeat a specific behavior, perfectly, on cue. Behavior that deviates from the goal is considered a mistake to be overcome. By most standards Grimmy's behavior is substandard. The trainers at Hawaii's Sea Life Park may not share that view.

About 20 years ago, Karen Pryor, the co-founder of Sea Life Park, and Ingrid Kang, her head trainer, made a revolutionary discovery. They had introduced a feature in one of their dolphin shows that gave the audience a peek into how behaviors are shaped and controlled. They expected it to give the visitors an exciting glimpse of how animals learn—but it wasn't the audience that received the biggest shock.

Malia, an adult female dolphin, was brought into the tank from a holding pen. Instead of the regular hand signals and cues she could normally expect, Malia was given no clues as to what she was expected to do. After two or three minutes of swimming she slapped her tail impatiently on the water. Ingrid tossed her a fish. This was something Malia understood. She slapped her tail repeatedly throughout the show.

For the next show Karen and Ingrid were faced with a new problem. Since the slapping behavior had been reinforced, Malia automatically offered it when she was allowed to choose a new behavior. They wanted each audience to see what it is like to reinforce a new behavior. They decided to reinforce Malia for any behavior other than tail slapping. This time they got a Flipper-style tail-walk.

After a few days, the trainers had exhausted Malia's bag of tricks. They had consistently reinforced her for doing different behaviors at each performance. The trainers were at a loss as to how to get new behaviors for every show. Malia solved the problem for them.

In the next show, Malia tried offering some of her old behaviors to the trainers. She slapped her tail and walked on her tail and swam upside down. The trainers refused to reinforce these previously established routines. Frustrated at not getting any fish after all that effort, Malia tried one last thing. She flew out of the water in what looked like a typical jump. This jump had one important difference—Malia was upside down. The trainers were stunned. Dolphins do naturally jump out of the water, but not on their backs. Malia had never been taught to do this behavior. The answer was both obvious and incredible. Malia had "created" a behavior! This chance discovery lead to a serious scientific research project and many new insights. The weeks that followed proved conclusively that humans are not the only animals capable of creative behavior.

One important discovery was that many types of animals are capable of "creating" behaviors. A subsequent project used pigeons as the subjects of the experiment. The conclusion was that even bird brains can develop new behaviors—behaviors that would be almost impossible to teach. Like lying upside down, or flying two inches off the ground and staying there.

All of the animals used in the research seemed to enjoy training more when they had an opportunity to innovate. They consistently went beyond the expectations of their trainers and offered previously unheard of behaviors. While formal training has its place, evoking an animal's creativity can be an exciting and rewarding experience. Rewarding novel behavior can expand your pet's horizons while promoting a mentally healthy environment.

As for Grimmy, the cockatiel, I tell him that he is a good boy for "improving" on Beethoven. His latest version of Beethoven's Fifth Symphony bears a striking resemblance to "The Camptown Races." Da-da-da DOO DAH! Now if he could only do something about Rap music.

Primarily, secondary reinforcers end on a good note

Ming, the Greyhound, likes to play fetch with her master, Bill. She runs swiftly for any object that he tosses—and then refuses to bring it back to him. She has the same problem when he calls her to come. She makes a good start but fizzles out before she gets back to him. Bill can't figure out why she will not respond. The solution is simple but subtle. Bill must stop encouraging Ming to come, and start reinforcing her for coming.

You may wonder how encouraging the dog to come could possibly stop her from performing the behavior. The secret to this puzzle lies in understanding how praise and encouragement work to change behavior.

When a sound is linked to an actual positive reinforcement, such as food or physical affection, it takes on all or part of the power of the actual reinforcer. Ivan Pavlov's research at the beginning of this century confirmed this phenomenon. He linked the sound of a bell to the presentation of food. Soon the dog would start to drool at the sound of the bell—even if no food was present. While the bell was not the actual food that the animal craved, it had the power to trigger the same complex reactions in the dog. When a sensation is associated with an actual reinforcer, this way, it is called a secondary reinforcer.

This information was a novel piece of trivia until the 1930s, when B.F. Skinner showed the world the power of these associations. Skinner proved that you could do much more than make dogs drool with a secondary reinforcer. He discovered that while the actual food reinforcer strengthens the odds that a behavior will occur, the secondary reinforcer is critical to telling the animal which behavior should be strengthened.

For instance, when Shamu is learning to do a back flip it is impossible to shove a fish in his mouth (the actual reinforcement) at the exact instant he performs the behavior correctly. Instead, the trainer blows a whistle (the secondary reinforcer) that means "YES! I liked THAT!" The whistle bridges the gap from the instant the behavior occurs to the time it takes for the animal to receive his actual reward.

While this may seem like a lot of psycho-babble, the correct application of this theory can have big benefits in practice. Bill's problem with Ming is a good example of the misuse of secondary reinforcement.

When Ming gets the ball, Bill attempts to encourage her by saying "Good girl," and "Way to go!" To Ming, the sounds of "good girl" and "way to go!" mean that she has done something correctly (get the ball), she can expect some kind of reward, and that the behavior is over. This is like the whale trainer's whistle. She translates the praise exactly as Shamu translates the whistle. (YES! I liked THAT!)

Because Bill does not understand how secondary reinforcers work, he has no idea of why Ming will not return. The first problem is with his timing. Bill's timing of the praise has consistently been at the instant Ming starts to come back. When he says good girl, she thinks she has been reinforced for picking up the ball—only! Since the behavior of returning has not yet occurred, she cannot understand that Bill is trying to reinforce that behavior as well. Bill has inadvertently reinforced her for starting the behavior, but not for finishing it.

To solve the problem, Bill must wait until the behavior is finished before he praises her. His mistaken belief that chanting encouragement will cause her to return to him has actually reinforced her for staying away. A quick solution will be to wait until Ming is very close to him and say "Come." Then Bill offers her a very palatable treat. He waits until she has come as close as she is going to and then says "Good girl"—at the end of the sequence. After a few repetitions she will be able to respond to his command by returning all the way. By giving her an accurate indication of what she must do to be reinforced, he will counteract his previously ineffective training.

Praise and encouragement are powerful tools for changing behavior. Correct timing is an important factor in using them correctly. If an animal has trouble finishing a behavior, try this unlikely advice—make sure you start with a good ending.

How to teach right from "wrong"

Fred, the Irish Setter, used to get yelled at frequently. The most common word that he heard was "No!" Whenever he heard it he cringed in terror.

His owners, the Lamberts, had difficulty training Fred because they had no way to tell him that he made a mistake. If they said "No" he would run and hide in the corner and refuse to work.

When an animal is learning something new, it will make errors. In Fred's case, errors were met with serious disapproval. Though his owners did not actually harm him, the association of the word "No!" with punishment was so strong that it shattered his confidence. If the Lamberts ignored the errors, however, Fred learned the behavior incorrectly. This contradiction ruled Fred's training until ultimately the family quit training him altogether. The family sensed that unless they could figure out this puzzle, Fred wasn't going to be in the family for long.

The Lamberts finally solved their problem in an unlikely place—the carnival. While Mr. Lambert was walking down the midway, one of the barkers cajoled him into tossing a softball at a stack of metal milk bottles. If he could knock them down, he would win a giant teddy bear. Mr. Lambert threw the first ball — and missed. Instead of yelling at him and calling him a loser, the carnie said, "Ah, gee, mister, that was sooo close. You almost did it. You ought to try it again!"

Mr. Lambert was shocked. He suddenly realized what Fred's problem was. The Lamberts had been trying to communicate to Fred that he had made an error and "ought to try it again." What they had really taught him by saying "No!" was to avoid the behavior entirely.

Mr. Lambert realized that he needed a gentle way to tell Fred that he had made a mistake. He decided to use the word "wrong." Every time Fred made a minor error, Mr. Lambert would say "Wrong" in a normal tone of voice and ignore Fred for a minute. Sometimes he would leave the room for awhile after using the word.

Soon, Fred made an association between the word and its consequence. He found out that if he heard the word "wrong" he could expect to be ignored for at least 30 seconds. The affection and attention that he wanted was removed when he made an error. Instead of cringing in terror, Fred would get excited and try the behavior again. Mr. Lambert had found a very powerful and useful tool.

After a few sessions, Mr. Lambert was convinced that his tool was a good one for simple obedience behaviors. But what about more complex behaviors? He decided to try it on an especially irritating problem. Fred always jumped on guests who entered the Lambert home.

First, the Lamberts invited a friend to come to the house and ring the doorbell. The friend was instructed that if he heard the word "wrong," he was to immediately leave the house. As the friend rang the bell, Fred leaped to his feet and raced to the door. He pranced and jumped against the door as he waited for Mr. Lambert to let in the guest. This time, Fred was in for a big surprise—Mr. Lambert did not open the door, he just said "Wrong" and went back to the living room. Fred watched as the guest walked around the garage and disappeared from sight. Fred was stumped.

A few seconds later the doorbell rang again. Fred attacked the door again. Again he heard the word "wrong" and the friend left again. This was not Fred's idea of a good time. He had to figure out what was happening.

On the next attempt, Fred changed his plan. He remembered that he had heard that awful word just as he started to jump up. He decided to fool his owner this time—by not jumping up! This time, the guest actually entered the house before Fred attempted to jump. Several more attempts and Mr. Lambert was able to switch from "wrong" to "good boy" and give Fred a treat for sitting, instead of jumping. Fred was delighted that he had tricked his owner into giving him treats for simply sitting by the door.

Most animals are willing to work for their owner's attention and affection. Withholding praise can be a powerful and humane tool for teaching your pet. Before you assume that punishment is the only means of correcting mistakes, make sure your pet knows right from "wrong."

What you teach is what you get

Biff is a smart dog. He has learned how to please his master, Jim, perfectly. Every time he hears a command, he dutifully ignores it for 30 seconds. After waiting patiently, Jim gives the command again and this time it's louder. Biff ignores the second command as well. By the time Jim gives the third command, he is screaming so loudly that he is in danger of shattering crystal. That's when Biff finally obeys the command.

Repeatedly yelling commands is probably the most common training error. If Biff does not respond instantly to a cue, he hears Jim say it again. This repeating of signals means that Biff can safely ignore the first few requests and still get treats and affection. Before criticizing Jim, it may help to know how this behavior developed.

Humans are capable of conceptual thought and the ability to communicate through speech. The assumption that these two abilities are connected is often unjustified. We often say things because we have been reinforced for saying particular words in similar situations—not because it is intelligent to do so.

Several years ago, my wife and I were visiting a drive-thru wild animal park near Seattle. A female elk tried to stick her head into our car—a small convertible sports car. The animal's huge head squeezed between the window and the cloth top. I automatically shouted "No!" My wife burst into laughter. The elk continued her assault. I yelled "No!" even louder. The elk finally pulled her head from the window when I moved the car gently forward. My shouts had no effect on the elk, yet I had yelled again—without thinking. The reason for this reaction is simple but not obvious. I repeated myself, not because I "knew" it would affect the elk, but because it had worked to stop other animals in the past.

When we speak, we assume that our words will be understood. If a person does not respond to our speech, we assume that he has not heard us and we automatically repeat the phrase. If this second attempt succeeds, we will continue to repeat in similar situations. As long as everyone speaks your language, repeating yourself will succeed. What if the person is a foreigner who does not speak English? If you say a word louder, or twice, you will fail to communicate unless the listener already knows the word. That's where Jim made his mistake—Biff doesn't speak English.

In the early stages of teaching Biff to lie down, Jim followed tradition and chanted "Down-down-down" as he forced Biff to the ground. Jim was not aware that he was saying the word several times on each repetition of the behavior. Biff automatically connected all three repetitions of the command into one signal. As Biff learned the behavior, he sometimes miscounted and lay down on the first or second repetition of the cue. Jim believed that Biff "knew" how to lie down because of these responses. Biff thought of them as mistakes. Soon Biff and Jim developed a consistent pattern. Jim would command "Down" and wait a few seconds. Biff thought "OK, one down and two to go!" Biff would hold his position perfectly, waiting for the next signal. Jim would get frustrated that Biff was still sitting. He would say the command again, "Down!"—this time a little louder. Biff would think, "There is number two. One more to go!," and hold his position. Finally Jim would scream the command with exasperated force. "DOWN!!!" Biff would obediently lie down. He was secure in the knowledge that he had performed the behavior exactly as his master had taught him.

In nature, wild canines survive by using their acute senses to their fullest potential. They must respond instantly to the first indication of a tasty rabbit or a hungry cougar. To take full advantage of your pet's potential, remember, say it once and say it softly. It's a no-no to say it twice-twice.

Searching for a fun behavior can be an end in itself

In the 1950's, many Saturday morning action television shows featured a dog companion. From Sky King to Roy Rogers, canines were integral parts of the plots. The most worn out gimmick usually required that the hero be wounded, trapped by a log or in some way immobilized. Then Roy, Timmy or Sky would command, "Find Dale," (Gramps or Penny—take your pick). Off like a shot, the faithful dog would unerringly bound across the prairie, desert or farm until finding the person, barking and pulling their shirt sleeve. It is amazing that it always took the tugging before Dale, Gramps or Penny figured out that the dog wanted them to go someplace.

While actual tracking dogs work with a little less drama and a lot less racing across the prairie, they often perform amazing feats of smell. The sense of smell, called olfaction, is so keen in dogs that researchers have difficulty making machines accurate enough to test it. While past studies have proven a dog's ability to discriminate compounds at about one part per two million (which translates to a literal "drop in the bucket"), a current study at Auburn University is utilizing a machine designed to present scents at one part per billion. It is believed that some dogs can detect certain smells in quantities as small as a few molecules. To duplicate this feat, a person would have to be able to find a particular needle by searching every haystack in Kansas.

While some dogs appear to be more capable of discriminating scents than others, most dogs are capable of remarkable scent discrimination. The quickest way to find out if your dog has "star quality" is to teach him to find someone using the secret TV dog training methods of Roy, Sky and Timmy. Whether you use this in play, for sending notes back and forth, or as a practical emergency measure, developing your dog's tracking abilities can be a rewarding experience.

First, make sure your dog knows how to come when called. If Fido is ignorant about this behavior, you can teach it quickly. Get some treats and rub one against the dog's nose so that he knows what you have. Turn your back to him and say "Come." If he still balks at this scenario, place the treat on the ground between your feet. Just before he grabs the treat, say "Good." Repeat this until the dog is fascinated with the process. Add a second person to the game. Stand about five feet apart and take turns asking him to come.

Next, select the person you wish to be the target. As Fido comes to you, say "Find Mom"—or Dad, or Billy, etc. Then have the person command "Come." When Fido goes to the other person, he should get praise, affection and treats (get him very excited.) The target person can then command the dog to find you. You then say "Come." Soon the sound of each person's name will identify that person. Fido will be able to understand the difference between Bill, Mom and Dad. Gradually have the person move slowly away from you, moving a few feet farther on each repetition.

Once Fido can find the person with ease, the next step in the process is to block the dog's path with a visual barrier. Have the target person enter a room and close the door. As you command "Find Billy," the dog will race around in frustration. If his visual abilities are incapable of solving the problem, he will automatically switch to sound and scent as clues. You may have to command the dog again to find the person as the dog becomes frustrated. If the dog fails, have the target person open the door and ask the dog to come. Continue with this until the dog can understand the process of "hide and seek."

After developing the behavior of finding a person in the house, it is a short step to repeating the behavior in a park or wooded area. Have a family member walk through the park and hide behind a building or other obstacle. Make the first searches easy, and gradually get more complex. Make sure to give Fido lots of praise, affection and treats for success, but no punishment for failure. The idea is to make finding someone a wonderful game.

Monique, the "One Trick Poodle"

Monique, the Poodle, knows how to sit. She sits when you ask her to sit and when you don't ask her to sit. She will also sit when you ask her to lie down and when you ask her to speak. When you ask her to come, she will run slightly out of your reach and then sit—just far enough away so that you cannot grab her. Though this behavior may not appear intelligent, Monique is actually a very bright dog.

Before you can appreciate Monique's intelligence, you must realize that she behaves this way, not because she is stupid, but because this behavior "works." Whenever she is asked to do anything, she stands a good a chance of being rewarded by performing her favorite behavior—sitting. This pattern is the result of a long standing family tradition. Her owners are convinced that Monique is cute, no matter what she does. When they ask her to sit or lie down, they never really pay attention to whether she performs the desired behavior or not. They laugh and cuddle her and joke that she is "brain dead." This lackadaisical attitude has taught Monique an important rule for living with her human companions—when in doubt, sit.

Many pets have adapted to their surroundings exactly as Monique has. If they are not required to perform precisely, they don't. If they are expected to perform behaviors without being taught how to do them correctly, they eventually quit trying and fall back on behaviors that have succeeded in the past. Trainers who decry the stupidity of such animals are missing a major rule of training—animals do not intentionally fail. Most often their failures can be directly linked to poor training or improper reinforcement.

Avoiding this problem starts with realizing that only a tiny percentage of dogs are truly "brain dead." The vast majority are capable of better performance than they usually offer. They simply need to know that there is a benefit that comes from precise performance. If you can find something your pet is willing to work for, such as treats, toys or affection, you can find out your pet's true potential.

A good place to start is with the behavior "sit." Almost every adult dog knows a version of this behavior. Get a handful of treats and call your dog. Ask Fido to "sit" and count to two. If Fido does not drop his buns to the floor within two seconds, turn your back on him and walk a few feet away.

A few repetitions of this and Fido is momentarily puzzled. In the past, all he had to do was lazily sit after the third or fourth command and he still had a good chance for a reward. Suddenly the game has changed. To his amazement, he realizes that there is a time factor to this new game. If he doesn't respond instantly, he loses his chance for reward. Fido smiles at this thought. This is something he can really understand. His wild ancestors never had two or three chances to slowly chase a rabbit. He may be a domesticated dog, but he knows about instantaneous reaction to cats, letter carriers and joggers. Fido wakes from his fog and sits quickly on the next repetition. You congratulate him with verbal praise and give him a treat. Move to a new location and try it again. Begin to raise your standards for any behavior that Fido knows how to perform. If he is inattentive, walk away and ignore him for a few seconds.

Expanding this exercise to other areas of Fido's life is simple. Start asking him to perform a behavior before you pet him. Ask him to sit or lie down before you give him a meal. If the behavior is not done well, turn away and ignore him for a while.

This simple process of expecting a dog to "work for a living" is the first step toward getting better performance from your pet. If you reinforce a dog for sitting when you asked for "down," or repeat commands many times, you are teaching poor behavior. Teaching Monique and Fido that they can get affection and treats in exchange for minimal performance will undercut any control you may currently have. Your new approach to training will develop responsive and enthusiastic performance. Your pet will also gain a reward far bigger than a food treat—an occupation.

Part 2:
Problem Behavior

Live long and vegetate!
Dying of boredom

Dogs, in the wild, rarely live past six years of age, but a well-kept city dog may easily live past twelve. Wild cats rarely make it to four or five years of age, while a house cat can live to be 18 or 20. One might think that with all the nutritional and medical tools available for helping our pets live longer, they would automatically be happy critters. The truth is, that for most of those extra years, the animals are virtually bored to death.

Life in the wild is a short and exciting experience. Never knowing when a predator might be sneaking up on you will certainly keep you alert. For wild animals, just staying alive makes bungee jumping look tame. Nature offers an often meager existence for successful animals and sudden death for the unwary.

Captivity, however, is not so kind. On the surface, life with humans appears to be a cushy job. Get up in the morning, eat breakfast, go back to sleep for several hours, bark at the neighbor, go back to sleep, wait for dinner, jump on the dining room table, go back to sleep, jump on mom and dad when they get home from work. Even by the simple standards of dogs and cats, there comes a day when this routine gets old. There are only so many ways one can go to sleep, and we humans are so slow that playing keep-away with dad's favorite slipper eventually loses its appeal.

The side effects of living in this "mild kingdom" can be equally dangerous as life and death struggles in the wild. Bored, energetic pets are prime candidates for getting into mischief. When an owner returns home to find a $1000.00 couch reduced to coiled springs and wisps of cotton, someone is likely to go to the animal shelter—pronto.

Another favorite boredom-related behavior is senseless, random digging. When a dog digs huge craters in the backyard, it is often a plea for mental stimulation. Whether the dog is digging to escape, or simply attempting to recreate a lunar landing site, the cause is the same. Cats occasionally participate in unearthing house plants as a form of entertainment as well. A common feline wrinkle to this occupation is to knock the plant off a shelf while it is still in the pot.

A sure sign of boredom is an obsessive fascination with every bird, bug or sound that enters the back yard. For dogs, this is often accompanied by chronic and prolonged bouts of barking and howling. In a never-changing environment, even making noise is a diversion.

One of the first steps toward curing an animal's ho-hum existence is to make it slightly different each day. If a dog or cat has favorite toys, they can be hidden around the house or yard to encourage "search and find" missions. (Can't tell if Fifi or Felix plays with toys while you are gone? Place them in a geometric pattern like a square or star and observe them when you get home. This is a good way to find out which toy is the animal's favorite, and which are not being played with.)

Obedience training can be a wonderful way to get your dog to use its brain. Besides traditional training, there are now many other organized forms of training that can be of benefit. Schutzhund is a German form of training that also includes teaching your animal to protect you. Field trials are for sporting dogs like pointers and retrievers, while herding competitions are becoming a common event in urban as well as rural areas.

Tracking events are also a fun and mentally grueling adventure for the common pet. Mixed breeds and purebreds alike can derive benefit from this challenging task. Whether the tracking is at a formal competition or just teaching Fido to find your children, it can solve the boredom factor in your dog's life. If your dog has a knack for scent discrimination, you may consider joining a local search and rescue organization and participate in actual rescues of lost or missing people.

Perhaps the most intriguing type of training and competition is a newcomer to the field—agility. Agility training is composed of a series of tasks the handler and dog accomplish while competing against the clock. As the name implies, the dog must negotiate a number of barriers and obstacles, such as running inside a long tunnel and over a narrow balance beam. Teams of handlers and dogs compete for the lowest time score.

While most owners are committed to providing their pets with the best nutrition and medical care available, they often neglect their animal's mental health. Whether an animal performs tricks or purposeful tasks, mental activity is a requirement for a long and happy life.

A look at punishment

The domestication of animals started about fifteen thousand years ago. Since that time, punishment has been the primary means of controlling these created critters. Over the centuries, many people have developed an almost superstitious awe of punishment, even though it rarely accomplishes the desired reaction. To understand why punishment is so popular and why it rarely works, requires a closer look.

The word "punishment" should not automatically imply thumbscrews or eye gouging. Punishment can occur even if no actual harm befalls the punished. A working definition of the term would be "the presentation of something that reduces the chance that a behavior will occur." For example, sharks can "punish" swimmers just by showing their dorsal fins. Hot rooms punish those who wear heavy clothing. Once the shark is removed, or the temperature drops, swimming and wearing heavy clothes will return to a normal rate of occurrence.

Punishment, therefore, decreases the likelihood that something will happen. To say, "I punished the dog for soiling the carpet" is inaccurate if the behavior has not decreased in its rate of occurrence. This practice of inflicting discomfort after the fact is more accurately described as retaliation or retribution, i.e., you may have inflicted pain or terror but the animal did not connect it to the behavior. By definition, when used correctly, punishment always decreases response. The problem is that punishment is rarely the best solution to a problem and is almost never practiced correctly.

The first rule of punishment is that it must be closely connected with the event that you are trying to punish. For instance, many cat owners face the problem of cats that investigate kitchen countertops. Most people wait until they see that the cat is already on the counter before they scold it. While this may terrify the cat at the moment, it will do little to decrease the likelihood that the cat will jump on the countertop tomorrow. The cat may associate you with the punishment and simply get on the counters only in your absence.

In order to decrease counter-sitting, the punishment must start at the instant the cat begins to jump on the counter, not after he has already gotten there. Here's a practical way to quickly extinguish the behavior. Go to a hardware store and get some thin, clear, hard plastic sheeting or Plexiglas. Tape the plastic sheet between the counter and the wall so that it forms a transparent slope. When Felix jumps upward, he is going to hit the angled plastic and slide off onto the floor. A few "alley oops!" and the cat will be permanently trained through safe punishment.

The second rule of punishment is to make sure that it is consistent and permanent. For instance, the dog that attacks the front door in response to the doorbell, is a common nuisance. To punish this wild and crazy behavior, simply start ringing the door bell before you enter your own front door. As Fido races toward the door he is expecting the mailman or an unknown visitor, and is gearing up for some wild barking. Instead of a stranger, there stands his master! A few well placed "punishing" words may be enough to instantly interrupt Fido's confidence. Over a series of repetitions, the likelihood that he will race to the door decreases and the behavior will soon disappear completely. (For more resistant pups, a blast from a squirt gun may be necessary to stop such a powerful behavior.) Once the behavior is eliminated, start giving Fido a treat for remaining passive when guests arrive. This will change his motivation and help to maintain his good behavior.

While these examples of punishment are relatively straightforward, there is a caution that accompanies any use of aversive control. The behavior you punish may not be the only one affected. You may wipe out a number of desirable behaviors unintentionally or create more problems than you started with. For instance, chasing small children is a typical but objectionable canine behavior. If you are expecting a number of small bipeds at your home, you may use balloons to punish chasing behavior. First, inflate some balloons and pop them in your dog's face. Once Fifi is totally appalled by the sight of balloons, simply pin one on each of the children. Fifi is not going to approach any "wee ones" as long as they wear the dreaded balloons. You have now successfully "punished" child-chasing behavior. If you think this sounds like a foolproof solution, think again. Your first concern may be that your dog may become afraid of all loud noises. Second, she may become afraid of children, and third, she may become terrified of balloon-like objects such as watermelons and cantaloupe.

Another difficulty with this type of training is that intentionally terrifying an animal is a justified stumbling block for many owners. Even though they may regularly punish and terrify the pet in anger, to do something in such a coldly calculating fashion is emotionally difficult. Ironically, it is the precisely executed punishment that is more effective and potentially more humane. Punishment may be reduced dramatically if it is used to disrupt behavior in concert with a program of positive reinforcement for correct behavior.

Despite the fact that punishment rarely accomplishes the behavior changes desired, some people retain an unrelenting belief in its effectiveness. Many pets are traumatized and ultimately ruined by failed rituals of punishment, retribution and reprisal. Before considering punishment to change your pet's behavior, ask, "Is it safe?" After punishing your pet, ask, "Did it work?" and "What was the cost?"

Sinking your teeth into destructive chewing

Joann came home from work today expecting to see her dog, Butch, eagerly waiting to greet her. Instead, Butch was cowering under a table trying to blend in with the carpet. Joann did not have to look very far to see that Butch had chewed up the TV remote control—again!

A common belief of pet owners is that their animal knows right from wrong. Since Butch "looked guilty," he obviously knew that chewing up a remote control was wrong.

Joann is convinced that Butch chews things out of spite. He always seems to pick items of special importance to Joann—but of little importance to himself.

It is understandable that she might feel this way. It certainly appears as if Butch is selecting items that are guaranteed to make his owner unhappy. But is he really choosing things based on his knowledge of what Joann finds valuable?

To start with, Butch was a very "mouthy" puppy. When his permanent teeth came in, he chewed everything he could reach. At first, Joann used an old tennis shoe to keep Butch occupied. Butch soon graduated to Joann's $75 aerobic shoes. Next, Joann used some flat rawhide chips that Butch loved to gnaw on. One day, as she slipped her shoes off and took a nap, Butch finished his rawhide chip and looked for a likely substitute. Joann's $60 leather pumps made a perfect appetizer.

Frustrated by Butch's destruction, Joann started leaving him in the backyard. Butch liked it at first, but that old desire to chew came back very quickly. Butch looked for a suitable surface for dental demolition. The drip irrigation system was the perfect answer. The black plastic had the same texture of softened rawhide. It offered just the right amount of resistance to give him a challenge.

Hours later, Joann came home from work and saw the damage. Butch approached her happily with wagging tail and slobbering tongue. Joann went nuts. She ranted and raved and scared Butch to death. She threw her purse at him—and missed. Butch hid under a lawn chair. After a while, Joann brought Butch in and apologized to him. Butch didn't understand any of it, but he was happy that the violence was over. The days that followed led to more destruction. After each incident, Joann got angrier and more violent. Butch tried to surrender by rolling on his back and cowering. He had no way of knowing why she was angry. Whenever she came home he would wait cautiously to see if she was angry about something.

Joann decided that Butch just wasn't paying attention. She started taking him over to any object that he had destroyed and scolding him. Butch learned immediately to avoid that object—when Joann was present. Later, when she was gone, he would investigate the object. He discovered that the things were never associated with punishment unless Joann was there. When he actually chewed the object, he always made sure that Joann was not around. If he had chewed one of these objects during the day, he would then be completely terrified when Joann entered the room after work. He did not know that it was the destruction that was bad, he merely knew that being in the same room at the same time with a chewed object and Joann was a bad idea. This look of fear is what Joann decided was guilt. Joann's attempt to connect the punishment with the destruction was futile. She thought that holding an object to his nose and punishing him would make him "realize" that chewing was bad. While this type of training didn't work, some of her other efforts were more effective.

By providing him with an old sneaker and rawhide chips she gave him a taste for shoes and leather. The plastic of the drip system was remarkably like the remote control. Rather than teaching him to avoid chewing, she inadvertently taught him what objects to look for.

Dogs are simple animals. In nature, they may dig, chew and bark with no ill consequences. The concept of monetary or sentimental value is completely beyond them. Their lives move from moment to moment with no thought of the future. Punishing a dog, hours later, will only teach fear and confusion—and looking "guilty."

Assuming that your pet is trying to make you angry is generally a mistake. Blaming the pet for the destruction will make you even angrier but will not correct the behavior. The first step in changing your pet's behavior is to change your own.

Flintstone's follies: extinction in bed rock

There is a scene at the end of every Flintstones cartoon that shows Fred putting his pet saber-toothed cat outside for the night. As Fred turns to go into the house, the cat darts back inside and slams the door in Fred's face. Realization dawns on our hero, and the show ends with Fred pounding on the door, yelling "Wilma!" at the top of his lungs. That, my friends, is a good example of an "extinction burst."

A basic rule of behavior is that if you stop reinforcing it, it will go away. Scientists call this disappearance of a behavior, "extinction." Ideally, you can eliminate many undesirable behaviors by simply deciding to ignore them. If Fifi likes to jump on you, start leaving the room every time she does. If Felix yowls at three o'clock in the morning until you let him outside, ignore it and the behavior will go away, right?

As with most "too good to be true" rules, this one has a catch to it. While withholding reinforcement will eventually cause a behavior to become extinct, few pet owners understand that initially it causes the animal to actually do the behavior more! As the animal's favorite behavior suddenly stops working, the critter escalates the behavior dramatically. This burst of activity occurs before the behavior actually reaches extinction.

To see this more clearly, lets go back to "Bedrock" and watch Fred's behavior for a moment. As the cat leaps inside the house, it locks the door. As Fred realizes that turning the door handle fails to open the door, he will wrench the knob harder and harder. Since normal door pulling has failed, he adds another behavior to it, yelling. His yelling starts at a reasonable volume and then escalates as it fails to bring Wilma to the door. Fred may pound and yell for several minutes before giving up. If the behavior has been especially successful in the past, he may rest for a few minutes and try pounding and yelling again. This time he will stop sooner. If pounding and yelling fail to cause the door to open, Fred will stop yelling and pounding eventually.

Now compare Fred's behavior with Skippy the dog. Skippy is a typical mutt who loves to jump on guests and lick them frantically. His owner, Ray, has started putting him outside rather than dealing with this unwelcome behavior. Skippy will then paw at the door until Ray lets him back in. It usually takes five paw strokes before Ray breaks down and lets Skippy back inside. Today Ray is going to stop the behavior by not reinforcing it. He has promised himself that no matter how much Skippy scratches, he will not let him into the house.

Skippy's first reaction to his isolation is the same as always. He waits about 30 seconds and paws delicately at the door. He then stands with his head cocked as if he is listening for Ray's footsteps. About a minute later he paws again. As usual, nothing happens. After the fifth stroke, Skippy senses that something is wrong. Ray has not opened the door. The dog strokes the door again twice in rapid succession. In a rapidly snowballing process, he starts digging at the door with reckless abandon. Ray has a very important decision to make. Skippy's extinction burst is so wild that he is rapidly ruining the door. If Ray caves in and lets his dog succeed, a new standard has been set. Skippy will simply paw five times and then dig madly at the door until Ray opens it. The extinction burst will automatically be incorporated into the sequence. Ray will have unintentionally made the behavior worse.

To solve this problem through extinction, Ray must be prepared for an even wilder reaction next time. First, he should probably tack some plywood or Plexiglas to the door to protect it. Then he puts Skippy outside as always. When the dog paws frantically at the door, Ray must grit his teeth and ignore the behavior. After the dog finally abandons the behavior from exhaustion, Ray must wait a few minutes and then invite the dog inside. If he lets him in too closely after the behavior stops, Skippy may think that the pawing worked. Several training sessions of this type will effectively remove the behavior from Skippy's bag of tricks.

Behavioral extinction is a good technique for humanely eliminating unwanted behaviors. While the principle of withholding reinforcement is simple, many people find it difficult to watch the behavior increase dramatically before it ultimately disappears. When you try this method to solve your pet's problem behavior, first, cut off the reinforcement, make preparations for the extinction burst that you know will come, and just let your pet yabba-dabba-do-it.

Puppy behaviors are best "nipped in the bud"

When Moose was a three-month-old puppy, he chewed up a shoe. His owners, the Schultzes, thought it was cute and laughed about the experience. They chalked it up to "puppy teething" and figured he would grow out of it. Besides, it was an old shoe. They would be glad when he was six months old and mature enough to go to "puppy class."

When Moose was four months old he started digging holes in the garden. Next he chewed up the sprinkler system and began jumping on guests. The Schultzes smiled and sighed and waited patiently until Moose turned six months old.

At five months of age, Moose developed a taste for garbage. He found that his increasing weight and strength could knock over the big garbage can to reveal the tasty treats within. He also learned to dig under the fence and knock down an assortment of garbage cans for a doggie smorgasbord. The Schultzes were becoming impatient with his behavior, but they were hopeful that they could soon start on Moose's training.

By the time Moose finally reached six months, the Schultzes enrolled him in a puppy class. He had swelled to more than 70 pounds and had become almost impossible to walk on a leash. His digging behavior had turned the back yard into a field of moon-like craters. The garbage can had to be placed on top of the kitchen counter to keep Moose away from it. The Schultzes had already received three warnings and a citation from animal control, because of Moose's expeditions around the neighborhood.

At the puppy class, Moose was the most unruly animal. The instructor did succeed in getting Moose to walk next to her leg—

barely. The Schultzes were somewhat able to control him, but only at class. Once they got Moose home, he reverted to being a big wild puppy. The trainer told them that they had to be firm and jerk Moose's chain if he tried jumping on them at home. When Mr. Schultz tried it at home, Moose seemed to ignore the correction. Mr. Schultz increased the force of the correction and Moose increased his wildness. He actually seemed to become more wild in response to the tugging. Mrs. Schultz had lost all control over the dog.

The Schultzes had even less success controlling Moose's other "bad" behaviors. A new fence kept him from cruising the neighborhood, but caused him to bark out of boredom. The trainer told them to put some pennies in a can and shake it in Moose's face to stop his barking. Rather than cringing in terror, Moose barked at the can. They were also told to keep the leash on him at all times. Moose wrapped the leash around a floor lamp, a chair and the kitchen table within the first fifteen minutes. The Schultzes reluctantly took the leash off in order to protect their furniture.

The fiasco with the leash caused the Schultzes to reluctantly decide to end Moose's public education. The "magic" classes had failed to solve most of his problems. Waiting until he was six months old had done nothing to insure his ability to learn proper behavior. Yes, he would sometimes walk on a leash, and come when called (as long as he was on a leash), but the suggestions the trainer had given them about chewing, digging and garbage had failed. Moose was out of control.

The belief that young puppies should receive no formal training is common. One reason for this lack of early training is the assumption that the puppy will shed unwanted behaviors as it matures. The concept that a puppy will "grow out of it" lulls many pet owners into ignoring problems that may only get worse. Chronic barking, digging and biting are all behaviors that usually increase in intensity unless they are intentionally modified. Some behaviors, such as protecting food or toys, can become disastrous if left uncorrected.

Scientific studies of early development indicate that puppies start acquiring learned behavior well before their first month of life. Modern behavior methods that emphasize positive reinforcement can allow owners to take advantage of their animal's early learning abilities. By presenting the pup with structured training, it can be taught acceptable behavior while bad habits can be nipped in the bud. The real issue is not whether your pup can learn and adapt to its new environment, but rather what and when it will learn—and from whom. Starting an early training program may well make the difference between a pet you can live with and a nuisance looking for a new home.

Spray paint and cat spray: pees in a pod

As I was driving on the freeway yesterday, I noticed that a new overpass had been completed. On top of the new paint was a smattering of highly stylized and unreadable graffiti. While nice people deplore graffiti and blame modern culture for senseless defacing of our cities, the behavior may actually be the result of a far more primitive drive—the instinctive tendency to mark the environment.

Many species of animals leave behind signs of their passing. Bears stretch as high as they can and rake the trunks of trees with their claws. If another bear finds the marks and can't reach as high as the highest marks, he will quietly mosey down the road to a location where he can be the tallest bear. These environmental marks act as a signal to tell strangers that the area is already occupied and will be defended.

Though the need to defend their territories may no longer exist, many domesticated animals retain this behavior. At about nine months of age, most male dogs begin to lift their legs and leave a few drops of urine on prominent objects in their territory. Urine marking, called micturition, is common to most male dogs and to some females. When a dog travels through new areas, it investigates the scents of other dogs and leaves its own.

Cats also use urine marking as a means of staking out territory. Rather than lifting their legs to place a few drops on a vertical object, cats back up to the object and spray it horizontally. Scent spraying among cats is primarily done by males, but may also be done by females.

For pet owners, the first step in dealing with urine marking is simply to identify the behavior. Many owners mistake common house training problems for micturition. Just because a dog lifts its leg to urinate, it does not mean that he is marking his territory. The main means of identifying scent marking versus regular urination lies in the quantity of urine. If you arrive home and find a small amount of yellow, pungent urine on your curtains, it is most likely scent marking. If you find a large puddle on the kitchen floor, it is a house training problem.

Unlike dogs, a cat's marking behavior is usually determined by the location of the urine and a sharp odor, rather than just the quantity. Cats prefer to spray on vertical objects such as walls, chairs, curtains and lamps. Though scent marking by cats is usually viewed as a purely territorial matter, cats with urinary disorders seem to have a higher likelihood of spraying.

Regardless of the cause, many pet owners find scent marking intolerable. Though many people learn to live with soiled walls, furniture and possessions, the majority eventually get rid of the pet or restrict it to outdoor living.

Because there appears to be a connection between male hormones and scent marking, surgical neutering is still the most effective way of controlling the behavior. Though neutering eliminates or reduces scent marking in a majority of dogs and cats, it is not a foolproof solution. A few animals appear to be unaffected by neutering, while others merely reduce the rate at which they mark their surroundings. Some mature adult animals with long histories of scent marking stop the behavior when they are neutered. Among animals that are neutered before puberty, some continue to mark their territory.

If neutering is unable to change the behavior, a veterinarian may recommend the use of female hormones, called progestins, as the next step. Progestin therapy may include a series of injections or regular doses of oral medication. Of those animals who are not effected by neutering, progestin therapy may decrease or entirely eliminate the behavior. The procedure is not without some drawbacks. Some veterinarians are hesitant to use progestins because of the possible harmful side effects.

Behavioral solutions as a therapy for scent marking offer limited results. Punishment, the tool most likely to be tried, is rarely effective. Rather than stopping the problem, the most likely result of punishment is to teach the animal to be sneaky and avoid getting caught.

A more effective treatment than punishment is the use of positive reinforcement for correct elimination. While scent marking and elimination are not identical behaviors, there appears to be a relationship between them. In a small percentage of dogs this method can be highly effective in reducing the problem, as well as causing the owner to focus on positive changes in the animal's performance.

The sound of one gene barking

Q: What do you call a Cocker Spaniel that barks 900 times in ten minutes?

A: Normal.

The question of whether a behavior is genetically endowed or learned is a common one. This "nature or nurture" issue has been argued by biologists, psychologists, ethologists and behaviorists for years. Has the Cocker Spaniel adapted to the environment, or is he simply responding like a pre-programmed robot?

In the 1950s two scientists set out to examine this question by studying the genetic basis of dog behavior. John P. Scott and John L. Fuller studied five pure breeds of dogs and tested them in 50 categories of behavioral reactions. After testing thousands of dogs, they discovered many interesting things.

First, dogs have plastic genes. That means that they are capable of great variations genetically while still producing fertile offspring. This allows for the obvious physical differences between Great Danes and Dachshunds. The genes that govern behavior are also capable of great diversity. Not only can this diversity cause differences between breeds, but it can also affect litters. Brother and sister may be close to identical, or completely dissimilar.

One of the easiest behaviors for Scott and Fuller to study was barking. While all dogs can bark, Basenjis, a breed developed in central Africa, are almost barkless. Though capable of barking, they rarely do. Scientists bred Basenjis to Cocker Spaniels to see how "barklessness" would be transmitted genetically.

They found that barking is a dominant trait. That means that if either of the parents possess the trait, there is a 75% chance that all of the offspring will also possess it. The importance of this knowledge for the average pet owner is obvious. If you are going to buy a Cocker Spaniel puppy and you don't see both parents before you buy, you may get one of those 90 B.P.M. (barks per minute) puppies.

Another factor in barklessness is that the behavior appears to be developmental. At different ages, the puppies bark at different rates. So, the 90 B.P.M. dog did not bark that much when he was 8 weeks of age. He probably started getting yappy at about four months—two months after he would normally be adopted. So when you pick a nice quiet eight-week-old puppy, you may yet find that you have the original "Barkmeister." That's another good reason for seeing the pup's parents before you buy.

This developmental aspect is a thorn in the side for puppy buyers and is ignored or glossed over by breeders. Scott and Fuller discovered that many behaviors do not develop until long after the animal is in its new home. Pseudo-scientific temperament tests for puppies convince owners that the pup's behavior is static and will not change for its lifetime. Scientific evidence points to the contrary.

Another aspect of development is the absence of some traits in infants that do appear later in life. Most people realize that male puppies do not lift their leg to urinate. The behavior "develops" at about nine months of age. Scott and Fuller discovered that other behaviors are also developmental. The quiet, submissive dog at the kennel may turn into a dominant, pushy bully. Territorial aggression and defensive aggression may not begin until after a year of age. Some dogs offer territorial aggression as early as six months, while others finally start growling protectively as late as two years of age. Other dogs do not appear to possess the genes necessary for this behavior, and will never be good guard dogs, though their litter mates may be.

One of the tests run by the scientists was intended to research what dogs would be like without human interaction. They decided to confine one family grouping of each breed in a fenced acre of ground. They observed the animals daily for a full year. Beagles, a breed that is often kept in large groups, lived together peacefully with hardly a squabble. Fox Terriers, on the other hand, actually killed each other in violent disputes. The implication of this information is that if you want to have many dogs living together in harmony, Fox Terriers would probably be a bad choice. Your best choice would be to have a pack of Beagles who would be likely to live fairly harmoniously together.

There is probably no other creature so identified behaviorally with its breed type as dogs. Scientific studies can reveal how much of the traditional view of a dog's breed type is correct and how much is mere superstition. Scott and Fuller's book, "Dog Behavior: The Genetic Basis," is a must for any serious student or breeder. Along with a good appreciation for the marvelous behavior of dogs, Scott and Fuller offer the reader the most powerful tool available for interpreting a dog's genetic tendencies—a grain of salt.

Fireworks and thunder

Sammy was a Siberian Husky that was taken to an animal shelter on the third of July. His owner told the shelter workers that he was moving and could not take Sammy with him. The timing was especially bad because the workers at the shelter didn't know the real reason Sammy was surrendered—the 4th of July.

On July 5th, after the holiday, the manager opened the shelter and took a fast look through the kennels. In Sammy's kennel, there was blood everywhere. There was blood on Sammy's silver coat and bloody streaks on the walls. His paws were dark red.

After a brief examination, the cause of Sammy's wounds was apparent— he had tried to dig his way out of a concrete kennel. He had scraped his nails until they bled. The night before, the town fireworks display had taken place at a nearby park. Sammy was so terrified of the noise that he frantically tried to escape his predicament. As the finale boomed over the gaping spectators, Sammy was suffering through the worst night of his life.

Fear of loud noises is a common problem for pets. In nature, the booming of thunder and the crack of a lightning strike are taken in stride. A wolf may hunker down under a rock or sit out a storm in a den or burrow. Animals that chose to run from the sound are rewarded eventually with peace and quiet.

In contrast, city pets are inevitably confined in some way. The loose confinement of a back yard allows Fido just enough room to get into trouble. As he darts frantically to get away from the noise, he is likely to claw through doors and windows to get inside the house. Fido may also choose to escape by digging under or jumping over a fence. It is not unusual for the animal to rip hunks of wood and sheet metal from gates and other obstacles. This blind, maniacal terror can lead to serious injury or death.

Once out of the back yard, the animal is especially at risk. Well-cared-for dogs have no skills at dodging traffic. Because most fireworks are shot at night, Fido is at greater risk because of limited visibility. Motorists will have a hard time avoiding a terror-stricken animal as it suddenly appears in their automobile headlights.

If the animal does survive the experience, deeply rooted fears may remain. Some dogs will ever after panic at the sound of a car backfire, while others tremble at the sound of distant thunder. Unless some action is taken, the terror is likely to increase in its intensity. The best way to treat this problem is through preventive conditioning.

The process of desensitizing an animal to loud noises is similar to that used by hunters. Gun dogs are usually introduced to cap guns and loud hand claps as puppies. As the animal grows, the magnitude of the noise is gradually increased. Soon Fido can handle the blast of a shotgun at close range. Pet owners can start by softly banging pots and pans together and escalate the noise gradually. Soon your dog will not be traumatized by loud noises.

If your animal already has an aversion to loud noises, the process of desensitization must be applied cautiously. Here are a few suggestions that may ease the stress of the 4th of July, thunderstorms and New Year's Eve.

- Use your stereo to gradually habituate the pet to loud noises. Modern CD players reproduce sound almost perfectly—guaranteed to fool Fido. Most record shops have sound effects CD's that include thunder, gunfire and explosions. By starting at a very low volume, the dog becomes used to the sound—a little at a time. As the dog becomes comfortable at each level of sound, turn the volume up a small amount. It helps if these training sessions include either playtime or meals. Distracting the dog through play can help desensitize it, while food can act as a mild tranquilizer.
- Discuss the advisability of chemical tranquilizers with your veterinarian. Contrary to popular belief, tranquilizers do not always calm an animal. Some animals actually become agitated when given tranquilizing drugs. A drugged dog that is terrified still can do a great deal of damage to himself. Ask your

veterinarian to test your pet's sensitivity to tranquilizers before you intend to actually use them. A dry run using a sound effects record is far safer than the real event because you can turn off the noise if the animal overreacts to the drugs.

- Some animals are best confined in a dog crate, or inner room of the house. The sound of fireworks will be softened partially by the walls. Dogs that become extremely agitated are capable of doing damage to their paws and mouth by attempting to dig and bite through the crate or a sheet rock wall. This method of confinement should also be tried before you leave Fido alone for the evening, while you enjoy the local fireworks.

- Another strategy that may solve the problem is to simply confront the issue in public. In some cases, the behavior will not occur in the owner's presence. Since most celebrations are outdoors, you may be able to take your pet with you without missing out on the fun. Make sure to use a slip collar, choke chain or harness that the animal cannot possibly escape, if you try this method. Obviously, if Fido slips his collar you are unlikely to catch him.

- Puppies should be conditioned to accept loud noises as soon as they are brought home. Breeders would do well to start the conditioning even before the pups are weaned. If the animal shows fear of the noise, drop your standards and move at a slower pace. Soon the pup will be able to withstand volumes normally reserved for "boom box" pickup trucks.

- Put lots of identification on your pet during summer storm seasons and holidays. Have the I.D. tag riveted to your dog's collar rather than using a flimsy split ring or "s" hook. Make sure you can get no more than two fingers under the collar so it will not slip off. Put a second collar on the dog in case the first comes off, or is removed by a person trying to call your number.

Alpha-schmalpha: When ethologists go bad

Max's dog, Goldie, bit his new girlfriend, Janet. Goldie had been chewing a rawhide bone and Janet had been cleaning house. As Janet bent over to move Goldie's bone out of the way, the dog bit her in the face. Max was enrolled with Goldie in an obedience class at the time and told his instructor about Goldie's behavior. The trainer nodded knowingly and said one word— "Dominance!"

Max listened intently as the trainer explained that dogs are pack animals and that they will often strive to dominate the pack. He said that Goldie was trying to exert her dominance over the new pack member. The trainer told him that to fix the problem, Janet must prove her dominance. Janet must roll Goldie on her back and pin the dog to the ground. "No matter how much the dog struggles," he said, "Janet must keep Goldie pinned down until she stops struggling."

Armed with this knowledge, Max told Janet the news. Janet was leery of the process. Max insisted that the only way to stop Goldie's aggression would be to force her to submit through "talking her language." Max won the argument, but Janet paid for his decision. They placed a bone on the ground in front of Goldie. When the dog growled to protect her bone, Janet grabbed her and struggled to roll her on her back. Janet succeeded in terrifying Goldie to the point that the dog was convinced that Janet was trying to kill her. Goldie bit Janet's hand, this time.

Max reported the failure to his trainer. The trainer passed it off as Janet's fault. He shrugged his shoulders and said, "She should have stuck with it. That dog is just trying to tell you she's the boss. You've got to dominate her or she won't respect you.

Tell your girlfriend to do it again, but this time don't give up, no matter what."

Max returned home and broke the news to Janet. He told her the trainer's conviction that Goldie would not stop biting her until she had been successfully dominated. Janet suggested that Max find someone else stupid enough to try holding Goldie on her back until she was correctly dominated. Max concluded that the trainer's advice sounded good, but Janet's perspective seemed to better fit the facts.

Over the last 20 years, the push to avoid harsh training methods has led some people to attempt to teach dogs "naturally." By observing the way wolves coexist, many assumptions are made about the way dogs respond to similar situations. Many trainers spend a great deal of time teaching ways to imitate a dog's natural tendencies of dominance and control. This is often compared to speaking the dog's language, or "talking dog." As Max and Janet found out, the holes in this theory matched the holes in Janet's hand and face.

There are two very important points to consider when discussing dominance and training. First, all dogs are not equally "wolflike" in their behavior. Some dogs, like Fox Terriers, are far more violent than their wild ancestors. They have difficulty living in large groups and may often inflict serious damage to each other. Beagles, however, can live in packs of 100 or more with little or no violence. To assume that all breeds react similarly to "natural" signs of dominance may not be valid.

Second, the way that humans attempt to mimic wolves is rarely an accurate imitation. If a wolf successfully dominates another wolf, the subordinate animal "gives up" by voluntarily lying on its back. Wolves do not grab each other with hands or physically lie on top of each other. For a human to grab a dog with his hands and force him to the ground is so unlike this process, it is unlikely to trigger a natural reaction in the dog. It is far more likely to terrify and confuse the animal.

Aggression and violence are both natural dog behaviors. Teaching a dog to be non-violent is an unnatural but necessary part of domestication. Using natural dog language to teach non-dog behaviors is usually a waste of time. Serious behavior problems like Goldie's require the correct use of reinforcement to effect lasting change. If you are faced with a problem of this type, consult with your veterinarian to find a qualified behaviorist.

Slices and bites :
dogs and pizza may not mix

Burt the Bouvier (pronounced BOO-VEE-AY) weighs about 100 pounds. His unkempt blue-black hair makes him look like a canine stand-in for Bigfoot. Burt is normally a very passive dog. He loves kids and other dogs and even strangers. There is only one thing that can provoke Burt to anger—when someone messes with his pizza.

Burt started out as a cute, fluffy puppy. He was satisfied with puppy chow and an occasional dog biscuit. His culinary goals were limited to food and more food. He looked so cute that the family often gave him scraps from the table. The family was unaware that feeding a dog from the table could cause problems. They didn't know that each helping of food acted to strengthen any behavior that Burt happened to be doing at the time he got the treat.

Soon Burt knew which behaviors worked and which ones didn't. Margaret, the ten-year-old daughter, liked to drop anything that she disliked on the floor. Burt gladly disposed of the evidence. If Margaret didn't have any surplus tidbits, Burt learned that he could still get "people food" from her. He knew that if he nudged Margaret's leg with his nose, she would often drop a snack. If that failed, he would grab her pants leg and pull gently. Margaret was the perfect victim of canine blackmail. She couldn't complain about the leg pulling without revealing that Burt was her partner in crime.

Of all the foods that he received, Burt liked pizza best. He was so interested in pizza that he took an active role in getting it. His favorite technique for pizza hunting was to wait until no one was looking and grab the pizza—box and all. Grabbing the pizza was only half the problem, though. Those pesky humans would chase him all over the house trying to get the pizza away from him. Once, when he was trapped in the kitchen, he learned that keeping the pizza for himself was simply a matter of growling and displaying his teeth. Burt's family finally realized that they had a problem.

Food stealing is a normal dog behavior. Wild dogs and wolves often squabble over their prey. Usually the arguments are resolved without serious damage on either side. The victor keeps the food while the vanquished waits for scraps. This natural order can easily go haywire when humans and dogs interact.

Burt's behavior started as a natural urge. His owners taught him that very palatable food was available at certain times, in certain locations. Burt easily adapted to the household rules by paying particular attention whenever the family gathered around the dinner table. Burt's use of aggression was a natural development. Since his human family was afraid to recapture the pizza, Burt learned that aggression works.

There are several ways to avoid food-oriented problems with your dog:

- Regularly remove items from your dog's mouth while he is still a puppy. Teaching him to drop any object, especially food, sets you up to be in control of him as an adult. If a puppy displays aggressive behavior, you have a better chance of controlling it while the animal is young. If the behavior persists, despite your efforts, seek professional help immediately.
- Refrain from allowing your dog near the table during meals. If Fido isn't getting scraps from the table, he will be less likely to compete with a family member over food. You also need to teach him to avoid investigating the table at other times.
- Require Fido to work for any treats that you give him. Unearned rewards will undercut your overall control of the dog. The fastest way to spoil a dog is to convince him that he will receive treats even if he does not obey.
- Teach your dog to avoid plates, cups or bowls lying on the ground. Guests and kids are notorious for laying bowls and plates in tempting locations. You can't control the behavior of every guest that enters your home, but you can control your dog.

Separation anxiety

Rudy, the Sheltie, has a rather interesting habit. Because of his habit, his owners, Rob and Nancy, confine Rudy in the laundry room when they go to work. When they get home, they look to see how much damage he has done while they were gone. Rudy's habit is driving his owners crazy. His habit is chewing through walls and doors.

As a puppy, Rudy had all the normal experiences common to young domesticated animals. He learned to eliminate outdoors and not to chew on shoes. He learned to bite softly when playing and to dance on his hind legs. For the first year of his life there was always someone at home to play with him. Then Nancy decided to go back to work and Rudy started tearing things up.

At first Nancy believed that Rudy was simply trying to get back at her for leaving him alone during the day. She felt guilty about leaving him and assumed that he must resent it. Certainly a human child could be spiteful if it felt neglected.

She tried to make up for it by lavishing attention and affection on Rudy when she was at home. Instead of correcting Rudy's problem, the extra attention seemed to increase the destruction. Nancy also began to notice another change in Rudy's behavior.

As she got ready for work, Rudy would start to pace anxiously. By the time she was ready to put him in the laundry room, he was frantic. Where once he waited until she left to start the destruction, now he began attacking the wall as soon as she confined him.

Nancy realized that Rudy's problem was not spite over being left alone—it was anxiety and fear. She also realized why giving an added share of affection had caused the problem to get worse.

Rudy's behavior was similar to the tantrums that young children display when they are separated from their mothers. Her pediatrician had called it separation anxiety. If Rudy needed to learn to be left alone, then fussing over him was the worst thing she could do. Rudy needed to be weaned of constant attention or he would never stop the destruction.

Her first step in solving the problem was to cut back on unearned affection and treats. She started refreshing his memory of the behaviors he had learned when he was young, such as sit, down and come. She began putting him in the laundry room for very short periods of time. She decided to include short isolation for times other than when she needed to go to work.

One of the first things she found, was that Rudy could tell the difference between the times when she was home, and when she was not. She thought carefully about it and decided that he had probably learned the sequence of events that consistently led to her leaving. She noticed that the sound of the garage door and her car door were loud enough to hear from the enclosed laundry room.

On her next day off, Nancy decided to try an experiment. She and Rob pretended that it was a work day and got ready as usual. Nancy turned on a radio near the laundry room to help disguise the sounds of leaving. Then she asked Rob to drive his car out of the garage and park it around the corner. His next job was to walk back and drive her car away, to convince Rudy that both of them had gone.

This time, Rudy was fooled. When he heard the second car leave he started to whine and scratch and bite at the door. This time things did not go as usual. Nancy yelled "NO!" and burst into the laundry room. She scolded Rudy and spritzed him in the face with a squirt gun and then immediately closed the door. Nancy's sudden appearance startled Rudy enough to suppress his frantic scratching and chewing.

The rest of the morning, Nancy remained in the house, quietly waiting in case Rudy's bad behavior returned. Even though he whined a couple of times, he did not scratch, dig or chew on anything. Nancy knew that one experience would probably not be enough to completely fix the problem. She planned to repeat the process the next day to give Rudy a chance to practice being good in the laundry room. She realized that the combination of gradually extending the amount of time Rudy remained alone and an occasional "surprise" would be the keys to eliminating his anxiety.

Distractions and habituation

Woody, the Airedale, is an extremely bright, three-month-old puppy. The other day his owners took him to the park for the first time. Woody became instantly stupid.

Socialization is the common term for teaching an animal to be comfortable in its environment. Socialization encompasses several topics, including habituation and conditioning. It is the weakest link in most training programs.

In nature, animals must be selective about what they respond to. If a wolf ran away from every grasshopper or bird that he saw, he could not survive. The wolf would be so busy running away from imagined dangers that he would never find time to hunt.

Dr. John Alcock, an animal behavior expert at Arizona State University, addressed this topic in his book, "Animal Behavior." He used the example of starlings feeding on the side of the road to illustrate this process.

"Examples of habituation are familiar to us all. Birds feeding along a roadside habituate to cars roaring past them. Starlings are especially adept at habituating to humans and their activities. They have been seen dropping down between speeding cars to reach a scrap of food lying on a freeway lane marker. Initially they surely flew away from the approaching car, but gradually this inappropriate reaction was suppressed to the point where habituated birds will ignore moving cars almost completely." A common mistake concerning habituation is to forget how specific and limited it usually is. The birds that won't fly away from a speeding car will fly in terror if a car stops or even slows down. A dog can learn to tolerate a specific cat, yet attempt to kill all others. Another form of learning that relates to socialization is conditioning. While habituation is a slow process, conditioning an animal can allow rapid adjustment to a new environment. Conditioning uses reinforcements to quickly effect a change in behavior.

Imagine that Woody has not eaten in 24 hours. He is then taken to a park where he normally acts like a Tasmanian Devil. As he starts his frantic barking and lunging at every bird, flower and child, his owner passes her magic wand in front of his nose—a hot dog. Woody leaves habituation in the dust and flies to Pavlovian conditioning at warp speed. Woody wants that hot dog!

Not satisfied with just distracting her wild beast, Nancy wants Woody to refresh his knowledge of a simple behavior. She attempts one that he always performs correctly at home. Nancy says "SIT." A cloud passes over Woody's face as he hears the echoes of this sound in his mind. He has heard it many times before and has responded perfectly. Suddenly, Woody is torn between focusing on all the lovely sights, sounds and smells of the park, or the hot dog. Woody sits. Woody's decision to sit in the presence of many distractions is the first step toward better performance.

Training classes in the park often promote socialization during training. The dogs become a large group of very distracted critters. A percentage of the group will be unable to learn because they are overwhelmed by the distractions. These animals will not benefit from the experience. Attempting to socialize the pet at the same time that he is expected to learn a new behavior is rarely efficient. Imagine memorizing the Gettysburg Address in the middle of a buffalo stampede. Socialization should be done as a separate process, after a behavior is fairly dependable in quiet surroundings.

Your pet's socialization should start as early as possible. You should consult your veterinarian about the age at which your pet can be safely exposed to strange dogs. Make a list of the places where your pet will be expected to perform, or at least feel comfortable. Fido and Kitty will need to feel comfortable visiting the veterinarian, going to the park and walking on a leash, near traffic.

Include a variety of situations for each location or distraction. I once trained a Cocker Spaniel who would respond to commands only at night. His owner, a nurse who worked the graveyard shift, had never trained him during daylight hours. Socialization is a required part of any training program. Teach your pet in a quiet setting and then gradually add distractions. Don't be angry or frustrated if your pet suddenly seems stupid in a new situation. I don't think very well in buffalo stampedes myself.

Pica: You aren't what you eat

Binky and Snooty have something in common. To look at them, you would never guess that they share anything. Binky is a large mixed breed dog, while Snooty is a petite Siamese cat. Though they do not look alike and belong to different species, they share an identical behavior—they both eat inedible objects.

The term for eating inappropriate objects is pica. While dogs often ingest things like rocks, wood, plastic and metal, cats usually stick to objects such as wool, cellophane and string. Though the behavior is fairly common, scientific studies of this subject are slow to give definitive answers as to its cause or cure.

A common assumption is that pica is the result of a dietary deficiency. While a connection between improper eating and diet makes sense, it is not always the case. Chewing wool is a behavior usually found in Siamese cats. At about the age of puberty, the animal begins to suck, chew or ingest bits of wool from socks, caps or blankets. The behavior does not seem to be related to the nutritional state of the cat.

A rare but equally odd behavior of cats is licking the chemicals on the surface of photographs. Some cats will lick photographic emulsion as if they were gobbling catnip. Crinkley cellophane is also a delicacy for some felines. In the absence of edible plant material, some cats go to great lengths to find any type of roughage. Yet, some cats that have access to a wide variety of vegetation still eat cellophane whenever it is available.

Dogs present an equally bizarre pattern of improper eating. Most dogs will ingest bits of dirt, paper or other debris if it is mixed into their food. This apparent lack of concern for what goes in their mouths leads to other things as well. Many dogs chew on and swallow rocks of varying sizes. Some dogs swallow rocks barely small enough to go down the animal's throat. Consistent rock eating leads to horribly disfigured and broken teeth as well as life-threatening intestinal blockages.

Wood chewing is easier to understand but just as dangerous as rock eating. The texture of wood is a favorite for teething pups and bored adults. While many dogs merely chew the wood, some do ingest it. City dogs often find decorative bark chips especially pleasing as chew toys. Rural dogs may choose unused fire wood or fence posts as favored delicacies. Wood fragments may lead to stomach and intestinal blockages as well as rips and tears in internal organs.

Perhaps the safest but most disgusting eating habit of dogs is copraphagia—the eating of feces. Copraphagia can be broken down into two varieties—the eating of dog feces, versus the eating of the feces of other animals. Dogs have a preference for the stool of cats—a source of undigested protein. Dogs that live near livestock often love cow and horse droppings.

The most common reason for improper eating is simple boredom. Alone in a back yard with nothing else to do, Binky may chew stones or wood, just to pass the time. Ending improper eating habits may require several levels of treatment. Some forms of copraphagia, for instance, may respond to vitamin supplements and dietary therapy. Exotic behaviors, such as eating sheet metal, are probably not dietary disorders and are more likely to be boredom-related. If you can relieve the boredom, the behavior may simply disappear or at least decrease in its intensity. Obedience training often has a major impact on boredom-caused behavior.

If your animal has unusual eating habits, your first step must be to consult with your veterinarian. If your veterinarian decides that there is no medical cause for the behavior, ask for the name of a qualified behaviorist to help you solve the problem.

Nothing to fear but fear itself

Susie is an Australian Shepherd mix. Her owners adopted her from the pound when she was about a year old. They tell people that she must have been beaten by a man in her first home, because Susie is terrified of men.

Molly is also an Australian Shepherd mix. She lives several miles away from Susie. Though their respective families do not know it, the dogs are litter mates. Molly's family adopted her as a puppy from the breeder—a single woman. No one can explain why Molly is terrified of men. They know that she has never been abused.

A common assumption among pet owners is that the primary cause of fear is abuse. If a dog or cat seems fearful, it is assumed that some person must have beaten the animal. That is not always the case.

In the wild, animals react fearfully to many things. This natural caution toward unknown or unusual things helps animals to survive. A wolf that was not wary about approaching a mountain lion would not last long.

Though dogs and cats have been domesticated for thousands of years, they still possess this feature. The exact degree to which a domesticated animal reacts fearfully is affected by a number of factors. Some of these factors are genetic, while others are the result of the animals' environment.

In the development of puppies and kittens, there are certain critical periods that govern much of the animals' behavior as an adult. At a given age an animal appears to be more sensitive to particular types of learning. Puppies, for instance, appear to be extremely sensitive to their environment between four and twelve weeks of age. If anything scares them during that time, they may become permanently afraid of that situation. If the pup is improperly introduced to a vacuum cleaner at nine weeks of age, it may forever be terrified of Hoovers and Kirbys.

Adult cats are also greatly affected by their surroundings as infants. Much of their behavior is affected by their age when removed from their mother and litter mates and introduced to humans. These factors are most noticeable in cats that appear to hate people or other cats. It may often be the result of meeting people a few weeks too late in their development or being removed from the litter too soon. Rather than being an automatic liability, these critical periods may be used to develop powerful attachments to particular objects, situations or people. A dog that is exposed to many types of people as a puppy will be less likely to be fearful of humans as an adult. If you want an animal to ignore loud noises as an adult, start desensitizing it to sounds as an infant.

Early exposure to a varied environment is the best way to adapt an animal to human society. Assuming that an animal has been beaten merely because it is fearful may be incorrect. Ironically, the opposite is more likely the case—when they really needed it, no one touched them at all.

A first look at house-training

Chipper is a typical yellow Labrador Retriever. He is playful, calm, protective and intelligent. As a younger puppy he learned things so easily that his family, the Schultzes, thought he was a canine genius. There is only one thing Chipper does not seem to understand. At six months of age, he still isn't house-trained.

Chipper's house-training problem began even before he moved into the Schultzes' home. His breeder raised Chipper's litter in a covered concrete dog run attached to her kitchen. The mother dog and pups had a sheltered pad and blankets for sleeping. Once the puppies could walk, they learned to follow their mother from the bedding to the concrete floor to eliminate. This process of sleeping on soft surfaces and eliminating on hard surfaces soon became a comfortable routine for the puppies.

When the Schultzes brought Chipper home at seven weeks of age, they began his house-training immediately. They took him outside frequently and told him he was a good boy when he eliminated correctly. They bought a large plastic "crate" and put a soft bed in it. Chipper slept in the crate at night and spent his days between the yard and the house. Everyone in the family was sure that he would be house trained in no time—everyone except Chipper.

Within a few days it was obvious that Chipper did not understand the Schultzes' idea of house-training. The pup would not eliminate in his crate where his soft cloth blankets were, but anytime he was loose in the house he would eliminate on the tile floors. The breeder's suggestion that they encourage Chipper to eliminate on grass sounded like good advice. The only problem was that Chipper refused to eliminate on grass but consistently used the concrete patio instead.

In desperation, the Schultzes tried to punish Chipper for his "accidents." When they found his urine or feces in the house, they would take him to the spot and scold him. Twice, Mr. Schultz caught Chipper in the act and shouted "No!" and rushed the puppy outside to the grass. On each occasion, Chipper seemed terrified by Mr. Schultz's sudden movements. Once on the grass, Chipper stared at Mr. Schultz in fear and tried to scamper onto the concrete patio. When Mr. Schultz repeatedly prevented this by placing the pup back on the grass, Chipper stood immobile and stared fearfully at Mr. Schultz. After about 30 minutes Mr. Schultz would become impatient and let Chipper back in the house. The puppy would invariably scamper off and eliminate in some out of the way location.

In order to preserve some type of sanity, the family found themselves keeping Chipper in his crate for long periods. As the confinement bottled up his natural playfulness and energy, he became increasingly wild when he finally got out of the crate. The family realized this process was ruining their relationship with Chipper.

What the Schultzes did not realize was that the fact that their puppy consistently eliminated on tile floors was both the riddle and the solution to Chipper's problem. The root of this problem lies in the way dogs develop in nature. A wild dog or wolf gives birth in a hollowed-out burrow called a den. For the first two or three weeks, the pups are unable to initiate elimination so their mother stimulates and cleans them by licking. At about three weeks, the pups begin to move around. During this time a remarkable physical and behavioral change takes place. Now that the pups have teeth, the mother experiences some discomfort while suckling them. She often leaves the den to escape their constant chewing. The pups instinctively follow mom out of the den, where they find themselves in another world. This place is not enclosed like the den, but is open and windy—it is the non-den. Their tired muscles soon weaken and they eliminate. The mildly pleasant sensation reinforces this behavior.

Because of the simple instinct to follow their mother, and their ability to learn through repeated reinforcement, the puppies soon want to eliminate some place other than where they sleep. If there are any sights, sounds or smells that are unique to the den, or the "non-den," the puppies will learn to differentiate between them. In Chipper's case, he learned that soft surfaces such as cloth, carpet or grass were "den" surfaces while tile and concrete were "non-den" surfaces.

Changing Chipper's behavior is easier said than done. The Schultzes must somehow convince Chipper that his early conditioning should be abandoned in favor of an opposite set of rules. The first step the Schultzes should take is to avoid any form of punishment or scolding—even if Chipper is caught in the act. Punishing Chipper for incorrect elimination is as pointless as slapping a baby for messing his diaper. Mr. Schultz's inability to get Chipper to eliminate on grass is partly the result of frightening the pup by grabbing him and rushing him outside. Chipper now assumes that if he tries to eliminate in front of Mr. Schultz he will be roughly whisked into the air and dumped on the grass. This also explains the puppy's tendency to sneak off and eliminate in out of the way places. Rather than risk Mr. Schultz's "air transport service," Chipper will try to hide behind a couch or leave the room to eliminate. The last thing he would do would be to give Mr. Schultz some indication that he needs to "go to the bathroom."

If the Schultzes still cannot get Chipper to eliminate in front of them, they can use the crate to increase the likelyhood that the behavior will happen. The crate works best when it limits Chipper's opportunity to have accidents and allows the Schultzes to predict when he is likely to eliminate. If they take him outside and he refuses to eliminate on grass, they should put him back in his crate for 30 minutes and then try again. If they stick to this routine, Chipper will eventually eliminate on grass, which gives the Schultzes chance to not only praise him, but give him favored food treats and affection.

Once Chipper is again willing to eliminate in front of his owners, he must be given many opportunities for successful behavior. Taking him outside after waking, eating and drinking will help the family focus their efforts. To assist this, Chipper's food and water intake must be monitored closely. A regular feeding schedule can help to predict the times when Chipper is most likely to have an accident. The Schultzes' veterinarian should be consulted about his new schedule to make sure that Chipper's food and water needs are properly satisfied. Along with monitoring his food and water, his owners should keep a notebook handy to write down the time and circumstances of each accident. Often a pattern of accidents will become apparent only because of good record keeping.

The fastest way of switching Chipper's behavior is to create an atmosphere of praise and affection for correct elimination. His problem is not that he cannot learn, but that as an infant he learned too well. With patience and consistency Chipper will learn what to do. Instead of focusing efforts on punishment for misbehavior, the Schultzes must use the most powerful tool for solving this problem—catch him doing something right.

More about house-training

Mugsy is a six-month-old Boxer. He's obedient, intelligent, faithful and loyal. The only thing he is not, is house-trained. At least once each day, he has an accident in a spare bedroom or behind the couch.

Mugsy's owners believe they have tried everything to fix the problem. Each time they find a spot where Mugsy has urinated or defecated, they dutifully drag him over to it and rub his nose in it and whop him under the chin. They read about it in a book about house-training.

Mugsy's owners just know that he is doing it out of spite. When they do take him outside they can wait as long as 45 minutes but he refuses to eliminate. When they bring him inside, he wets or poops as soon as he can sneak off unobserved. They say that Mugsy knows he is doing wrong because he looks guilty when they find a mess in the house.

When Mugsy lived with his mother and litter mates, he didn't have this problem. He could stop and eliminate anywhere he wanted to. He lived on an outdoor patio covered with outdoor carpet. When he was taken from his litter and came to his new home, it didn't take long to figure out where the bathroom was. The house had wall-to-wall carpet. It reminded Mugsy of the carpeted floor of the patio. Mugsy automatically adapted to his new environment by urinating on the rug—right in front of his new owners.

The family sat stunned, watching Mugsy's horrible mistake. The father reacted first and shouted "NO!" and whacked Mugsy with a newspaper. The father wanted to make sure that Mugsy knew that this behavior was unacceptable. Mugsy learned something quite different from the encounter, however.

Instead of learning to eliminate outdoors, Mugsy learned to avoid the father. Whenever he felt the need to urinate he would make sure the father was not around. When the father took him outdoors, Mugsy held his urine as long as he could. He was terrified that he would get whacked with a newspaper for eliminating in front of the father. Mugsy would wait until he got back inside and had an opportunity to slink off to the spare bedroom or behind the couch in the living room. The fact that he would inevitably get caught had no effect on Mugsy. Dogs are incapable of associating pooping in the morning with punishment in the afternoon.

Finally, the mother saw something that put a halt to the punishment. Her teenage son had purchased a fake rubber "Puppy Poop" at a joke shop and put it in the living room. Before she realized that the stool was artificial, she automatically went to grab a paper towel to scoop up the mess—exactly as her son intended. As she returned to the living room, Mugsy happened on the scene. He reacted exactly as always. When he realized that a human was in the same room with feces, he looked "guilty" and cowered under a table.

"You ought to look guilty, you bad dog," said the mother. "I've just about had it with your messes in the house!"

She was about to scold Mugsy further when she noticed that the poop somehow did not feel right. It was too light, and smelled faintly of rubber. As she realized the joke that she had fallen victim to, she realized something else. Mugsy had reacted to the poop exactly as if it were his. If Mugsy looked "guilty" over a fake stool, maybe the punishment wasn't teaching him what they thought it was.

When she told the father about her discovery, he didn't believe her. She offered to repeat the scene to prove her case. She placed the fake stool in the living room and then called Mugsy. The family was astonished at the dog's reaction. When he saw the fake feces, he instantly looked "guilty" and dove under the coffee table. No amount of coaxing could get him to come out.

The family had to admit that the punishment had not taught Mugsy to eliminate outdoors. It had taught him to avoid humans when he had to eliminate. That was why he refused to eliminate in front of them outdoors, and why he consistently eliminated in remote areas of the house.

The family turned Mugsy's training around immediately. They focused on ways they could reinforce Mugsy for eliminating outside. First, they started feeding him at regular times. If Mugsy didn't finish his meals within about 15 minutes, it was removed until his next meal. If they left the house they would confine Mugsy to the uncarpeted laundry room—a place where he was unlikely to eliminate.

Next, they started giving him special treats and affection for eliminating properly. It took several days for Mugsy to trust them enough to eliminate in front of a family member. Once he understood that eliminating outdoors caused treats and affection, Mugsy started looking forward to going outdoors. Now he sits by the back door and barks to tell them that it is time for him to go outside.

Vicks tricks—slick quick fix

Chet Ludlow was an old fashioned dog breeder. He bred, raised and trained Labrador Retrievers for over 30 years. Whenever Chet went hunting ducks, he would take decoys, dogs, guns, ammunition, coffee—and Vicks Vap-o-Rub.

For the last ten thousand years, dogs have been selected for particular traits. Hounds were selected for sensing game animals by sight or smell. Pointers were selected for the opposite— remaining immobile after they sensed a bird. Herding dogs were selected for chasing livestock, while guarding dogs were selected for not chasing livestock. While all this unnatural selection was going on, dogs developed some incredible specialties. From ultra-fast Greyhounds to keen nosed Bloodhounds, many breeds have become so specialized that training them can be difficult. That's where the "Vicks" comes in. Chet's dogs had great noses. Sometimes, while training or hunting, one of his dogs would get very interested in a strange smell—such as a female in heat. Chet would produce his Vap-o-Rub and smear a tiny amount on the dog's nose. Presto! No nose.

Chet's idea was simple. He figured it was better to have a dog that would pay attention without the use of his nose, than to have a dog with a nose who wouldn't pay attention.

Limiting a dog's senses can be an effective way of changing behavior. If you can identify the particular sense that is triggering a behavior, you can use that knowledge to good effect. For example, Billy Bob, the Basset, hates the sound of thunder. During the annual monsoon he is terrified by the thunder and tunnels through sheet rock with his teeth. His owners have found a way to successfully confine him to a bathroom when they are gone. They leave a radio playing to drown out the sound of the thunder.

Rudy, the Sheep Dog, has always hated letter carriers. He has ruined several front doors while clawing his way toward postal intruders. Rudy's owner realized that the sounds of footsteps on the tile outside the door were triggering the reaction. A piece of outdoor carpet solved the problem. My neighbor's Lhasa Apso liked to look out the front window of the house. When he saw anyone walk by, he would fling himself viciously toward the glass. His favorite perch was on the living room sofa. The neighbors stopped this behavior in an instant by moving the couch away from the window.

There are two parts to any behavior: the behavior itself and the trigger that sets it off. Each of these owners was observant enough to identify a single cue that set the behavior in motion. Since the animal did not sense the right cue, the behavior didn't happen. This method can also be used in dogs that have learning difficulties. Dogs that use their eyes to chase game, like Greyhounds and Afghans, should be taught basic obedience away from visual distractions. Once the behaviors are taught they can be easily transferred to more visually stimulating settings. If your dog is constantly distracted by the sound of children or passing cars, you can use a portable radio to mask the offending noises. Once you have control over some basic behaviors, gradually reduce the volume of the radio. Your dog will be much more likely to pay attention despite the distractions.

Learning to control your dog's highly developed senses can be a challenge. The same ears that warn your dog of an intruder may also cause him to bark hysterically at the wind. Allowing a dog to react instinctively may inhibit learning and cause unacceptable behavior. It's up to you to tell Fido what his nose knows.

A tale of misdirected aggression

Tom and Jerry are pals. They started out as two cute little puppies in the same litter. They were adopted by the same man at seven weeks of age and grew into 90-pound adult dogs. They still romp and play and share everything. The only thing wrong with their brotherly love is that whenever strangers come to the house, Tom and Jerry try to kill each other.

Their owner, Derek, dutifully wades into these free-for-alls and tries to separate the dogs. On several occasions the dogs have misinterpreted his actions and bitten him on the hands and arms. Derek can't figure out why the dogs would be so friendly and then suddenly attack each other. To get to the bottom of this, Derek needs to see this through his dogs' eyes.

One of the reasons dogs are so popular is their ability to protect their owners and their territory. In nature, wild dogs are often required to defend their territory against the attacks of predators. If one of the animals is alerted to danger, it will bark to alert the rest of the pack to the danger. First one dog and then another barks to spread the alarm, then moves forward toward the perceived threat. As the dogs move forward, they form a rough skirmish line facing the enemy. A critical piece of information regarding this behavior is that these animals are looking at the enemy, and are unlikely to look at each other.

One of the primary threats an animal can make is direct eye contact. In many species of animals, this hardened stare can freeze an aggressive animal and force it to seek trouble elsewhere. Some animals, such as tigers, have protective coloring based on this common trait. These big cats have round dots on the back of their ears to prevent other tigers from attacking them from behind.

In the wild, a pack of dogs may actually stop an attack by simply staring at the intruder. If the intruder gets too close, the dogs will attack in defense of their territory. Though this behavior is adaptive for the wild dog, a city canine may wind up in trouble because of it.

When city dogs get excited, they react similarly to their wild cousins. First they bark to alert any other dog within earshot. Next they attempt to move closer to the enemy. This is the situation that makes their instinctive behavior maladaptive. As the dogs race toward the threat, they are defeated by fences, furniture and other man-made barriers. This leads to two very dangerous reactions. First, the dogs become more and more aroused as they are prevented from getting close to the target. Next, the obstacles force them to race back and forth and mill around a gate, fence or door. As the dogs move around each other, they invariably make eye contact. This eye contact at close range, triggers an attack—even between brothers. If a human attempts to restrain either dog after the attack begins, a nasty bite is the most likely outcome.

The term for this problem is misdirected aggression. Though the animal has another, more pressing threat to face, it is unable to get at it. As the tension and frustration mounts, the likelihood that the animal will attack something increases. This is like blowing up a balloon until it cannot hold the pressure and bursts. Once the animal is in a state of frenzy, the aggression is an automatic knee-jerk reaction.

Treating aggression of this type should not be attempted lightly. One of the mistakes associated with handling such a problem is to assume that a pet will never bite its master. The very nature of this type of aggression makes it likely that the animal will strike out at the first available target, usually its owner.

Pavlov's cure for barking: ring a bell?

I once met an experimental psychologist who had spent two years researching the best way to teach a child to throw a ball. She had divided the behavior of throwing a ball into 17 separate criteria and analyzed how each child developed each part of the behavior. I asked her how well the children's accuracy improved over the course of the training. "Oh, we didn't have them throw at a target," she replied. "We didn't think of that."

About 90 years ago another scientist, Ivan Pavlov, studied the way dogs react to the environment. His most famous experiment involved ringing a bell and then presenting a dog with a plate of food. After a few repetitions, the sound of the bell alone would make the dog drool—even if there was no food on the plate. This seems like more of that impractical scientific stuff, doesn't it? What if I told you this information holds the cure for a dog that barks constantly when the owner is away from home? Suddenly the dry scientific stuff seems a little more interesting. If we find out that drooling dogs also happen to be quiet dogs, maybe Pavlov's research isn't so impractical after all.

In his book, "Conditioned Reflexes," Pavlov wrote that he would have preferred to analyze the way that dogs react to food by studying the drop in blood pressure, heart rate and respiration associated with digestion. He also wrote that during the early part of the century, no equipment existed to read these signs. Pavlov was forced to record the rate and quantity of saliva drops to indicate the strength of a food reaction.

The importance of this knowledge is subtle but powerful. If food can cause a dip in heart rate, blood pressure and respiration, it can be used as a mild tranquilizer. By itself, this knowledge is not going to stop Fido from barking. It is the second half of

Pavlov's work that pulls this together. Remember, Pavlov associated a bell with food. By recording the rate of a dog's salivation in drips, he could tell how strong the reaction was. If real food can cause 10 drips per minute and the bell also causes 10 drips per minute, then the reactions are equally strong; Fido's body cannot tell the difference.

Fido's owner, Rob, buys an ultrasonic dog whistle (his dog can hear it—his neighbors cannot). He blows the whistle and gives Fido a treat. He repeats this process 50 times per day for a couple of days. Soon the sound of the whistle makes Fido's ears perk up. Now the tool is strong enough to do some work.

The next day, Rob has a friend drive his car away from the house. Fido now believes that Rob has gone away. Within a few minutes, Fido would normally start barking, but this day is different. At exactly three minutes into his confinement, Fido hears the magic whistle. He is instantly alert and charges around to find his treat.

Even though no outward sign indicates it, some interesting reactions are taking place in Fido's body. Besides getting excited, Fido suddenly feels wonderful. The whistle has always meant fun and treats. In anticipation of food, his brain redirects the flow of blood to his stomach—drawing some of it from his head and limbs. Within a few moments, Fido decides to lie down for a while. He feels the same sluggishness that we associate with a big lunch. His normal urge to bark is the last thing on his mind.

A few minutes later, Fido is up and restless again. From his window hiding place, Rob sees the increased activity and blows the whistle again. Fido's reaction is identical to his first, but doesn't last quite as long. Each time the whistle is blown, the reaction will fall off a little more, until after about 10 repetitions the reaction is down to zero. Rob can blow the whistle as much as he wants and it won't work—for a while.

One of the interesting discoveries made by Pavlov, is that this type of reaction has the ability to regenerate itself. If Rob waits two hours, the reaction will recharge like a battery and be back to 100% strength. If the whistle is blown periodically, throughout the day, Fido's barking will drop to a very respectable "dull roar" within a couple of weeks. Instead of acting like a bored, anxious and noisy beast he will begin to take his confinement in stride. Rob can give a whistle to his neighbors to allow them to control Fido in his absence.

Using scientific principles for practical purposes can be a challenging but rewarding experience. Pavlov's research may not seem useful on the surface, but upon further examination, offers a humane and effective cure for a very common problem. If you find that "practical" training manuals don't offer the solutions you are looking for, try to find something that "rings a bell."

Submissive (EEEKKK!) urination

Julie's dog, Sammi, is a young, female Cocker Spaniel. Whenever Julie comes home, Sammi wiggles wildly in excited greeting and urinates all over the place. Usually Julie just cleans it up and tries to ignore the behavior. Sometimes Julie loses her temper and scolds Sammi. The scolding makes the behavior worse.

Julie's frustration is understandable. When she offers Sammi love and affection, the dog urinates. When she scolds or punishes Sammi, she urinates. The first step toward resolving this problem is to realize that it is completely natural. Urination while greeting or being punished is a common dog behavior.

For puppies, this behavior usually takes on one of two forms. Excitement urination is the result of infant muscles that simply cannot hold the urine when the pup gets excited. Sammi's behavior is partially excitement urination. She can get so excited when she sees her owner that she temporarily loses control of her bladder. The vast majority of dogs simply outgrow this problem as they become stronger and gain control of their muscles.

Submissive urination falls into a completely different category. Dogs have several behaviors that reduce violence between them. When challenged, a submissive dog must display some or all of these behaviors to show its lower status and to prevent an attack. Submissive urination is most commonly offered in this type of greeting. By wetting, the dog is merely acknowledging the other dog's superiority.

While all dogs are capable of offering this behavior, few are as consistent as Sammi. Whenever she perceives a threat, she eliminates before anyone gets the idea that she might have a dominant bone in her body. To her, this behavior is perfectly acceptable and required.

When friends come to visit, Sammi is worse than usual. If a guest attempts to bend over and "pet the nice doggie," it triggers the behavior. If someone rings the doorbell, Julie tries to scoop up Sammi and put her outside before she has a chance to eliminate in the house. It never works. When Julie bends over to pick her up, Sammi urinates again.

Fixing the problem starts with understanding what signals trigger Sammi's reaction. First, dogs assume that direct eye contact is a challenge. For a submissive dog, even a moment's eye contact is intolerable. Eye contact from above, indicating that the other creature is taller, heightens this reaction. For Sammi, a person towering over the top of her is guaranteed to cause a submissive gesture.

Another signal that canines perceive as a challenge is bending over and/or touching the dog's head, neck or shoulders. Dominant dogs often display their control by placing their neck, or a paw over another dog's neck or shoulders. When a human pats a dog on the head, a submissive dog perceives it as a display of dominance. The pooch is likely to roll over on its back and wet.

To change Sammi's greeting behavior, Julie needs to avoid those situations that instantly trigger urination. When she gets home she will generally ignore the dog for the first few minutes. If she is successful in not triggering the reaction, she will try some very calm words of greeting and gradually add physical affection over the next few minutes. After the physical affection, if Sammi still has not eliminated, Julie will say "good girl" and give her a treat.

The use of food for successful greetings is an important ingredient for success. Since physical petting may actually cause the behavior to happen, food as a reinforcement is a logical alternative. Another advantage of using food, is dogs have difficulty urinating and eating at the same time. The dog's response to the food competes with the urge to eliminate and strengthens the correct behavior.

Guests to the home should be encouraged to pretend Sammi doesn't exist. If they insist on greeting her, confine the introductions to outdoors. Barriers, such as kiddy gates, can allow Sammi to get used to a person's presence from a distance, before actually greeting them. While this separation reduces her tendency to eliminate at first sight, you must still eventually deal with the actual greeting. When you remove the gate, it is a good idea to discourage her from rushing quickly at people and jumping on them. This practice puts her in a position that is likely to trigger the submissive urination.

For Julie and Sammi, the solution to this common problem is a combination of things. Julie will reduce the likelihood that Sammi will greet people incorrectly. She will do this by asking guests to ignore the dog. Whenever Sammi performs a correct greeting, she is going to use food and limited affection to reinforce the behavior. She is also going to give Sammi some time to outgrow the problem.

Submissive urination is a normal and relatively common behavior of dogs. Because the behavior is a response to a perceived threat, real threats and punishment can only make the behavior worse. If you are faced with this annoying behavior, there is one easy way to solve it—pretend it doesn't exist and it might go away.

Ethologists guess about why animals do things

I was watching a nature program on television the other night. The narrator explained that wild canines raise the hair on their backs, called hackles, so that they look bigger and more threatening to their enemies. He also said that they bury leftovers, only to return later for a rainy day snack. Another juicy tidbit of information was that sometimes the top female dog in a pack will kill the pups of other females. The narrator explained it was because she knows that there is only enough food for one litter at time. Most of the narration consisted of explaining the actions of animals in terms of what they think, and why they do what they do. To quote my Grandfather Shedd, "It ain't necessarily so!"

Ethology, the study of natural behaviors, is a universally fascinating topic. Diane Fossey's study of gorillas and Jane Goodall's research into the behavior of wild chimps are good examples of the ethologist's work. While the ethologist is primarily concerned with observing and recording what animals do, there is also a powerful temptation to speculate about why they do things.

It is commonly asserted that wolves bury meat and bones during lean times in order to dig them up later when they really need the nutrition. According to most people, that is why Fido buries things in the back yard. In reality, studies of wild wolves indicate that only one cache in ten is ever reclaimed. Is it that each wolf has only a ten percent inclination toward recovering things they have buried, or is it that only one wolf in ten possesses the gene? The answer is, nobody really knows.

While guesses about these types of behavior are seemingly innocent, they can cloud our thinking when they are translated into practice. Some trainers suggest that because wolves bury things in order to dig them up later, dogs should be given a part of the backyard that is reserved for digging and burying things. Though the original concept is mere speculation, the pet owner may still allow Fido to make the backyard look like an artillery range.

Another behavior of dogs and wolves is to circle several times before lying down. The explanation most commonly given is that the animal is trying to mat down the grass underneath him in order to make a softer bed. The "softer bed" argument leaves a little to be desired. First, not all dogs circle, and dogs that do circle don't circle every time. Second, most dogs circle regardless of the surface they pick for sleeping. They often lie down on a hard, cool surface such as tile or concrete, though there is soft carpet a few feet away. Even if the circling behavior is an attempt to soften up a sleeping place, turning in circles a few times will hardly do the trick. If a dog really wants to soften the ground, he can use a far more efficient behavior—digging! In fact, when confronted with a soft cushion or bed, many dogs dig frantically before laying down. Again, the speculation about why dogs circle is merely a guess.

One seemingly unquestionable assumption is that dogs raise their hackles to look larger and thereby more threatening to their enemies. The problem with this explanation is that little dogs routinely attack dogs many times their size. What possible additional threat can a long coated Chihuahua convey by adding one inch to his appearance, if his opponent is a Great Dane? One might as well say that animals increase their blood pressure just before a fight, in order to appear "more pumped up" to their enemies.

One reason for our fascination with these explanations is the assumption that all behaviors are equally necessary for survival. In reality, nature is less "survival of the fittest" and more "survival of the survivors." When an animal reproduces, it passes along beneficial behaviors as well as some that may have nothing to do with survival. Wolves that circled before laying down may have survived, not because of the circling, but because they were bigger or stronger than their counterparts. Animals that raised their hackles may have also possessed genes that made them better able to digest carrion. Sometimes an essential trait may be linked to a behavior that "came along for the ride."

Studying animal behavior is a discipline that requires your interest and objectivity. The images of animals that we get from television, movies, magazines and books often exploit our interest while asking us to abandon our objectivity. If you sense that an answer seems too glib to be true, feel free to put your hackles up.

Part 3:
Cats, Cats, Cats

Spite and malice

Ziggy, the cat, likes to urinate on Marie's bed. Marie is sure that Ziggy is upset with her because she started working longer hours. She tries to give him more attention than usual, but he continues to urinate on the bed. Marie does everything she can to tell Ziggy that she loves him—Ziggy does everything he can to tell her that he has a chronic medical problem.

It is a common assumption that animals destroy things to get attention, or to spite their owners. Often the owner is so convinced that the pet is being spiteful that they never stop to consider more basic causes for bad behavior. Until Marie looks at it from Ziggy's perspective, the true cause of his behavior will be a mystery.

Ziggy's problem started several months ago when he developed a mild urinary infection. One day when he tried to use his litter box the experience was very painful. Unable to understand why he felt pain, Ziggy did what any normal cat would do—he decided to avoid the pain by avoiding the box.

Later in the day, Ziggy had to urinate again. Cats have a number of very important prerequisites for a good potty area. Ziggy had to find a surface that felt soft enough to grip with his paws, so that he could prepare his latrine. The house had hardwood floors and tile with a few area rugs. The rug in the kitchen was his first target. It hurt when he eliminated on the rug as well. He had to keep trying new surfaces to find one that did not cause pain.

Several days later, Ziggy was running out of places to eliminate. He had tried each of the rugs but they all caused pain. As his immune system fought the infection, the pain eased somewhat so he knew the litter box had been the cause. Each time he tried a new place, the discomfort decreased. He was almost at the point of trying one of the rugs a second time when he remembered another surface that would be perfect—the bed spread. The bed spread was the perfect texture to sink his claws into. If he closed his eyes it felt like soft earth. He sniffed it to make sure it was clean. Then he pulled the spread across an area using the same movements he normally used to prepare a small hole in the litter. After he urinated, he pulled the bed spread to cover the spot. He felt very little physical discomfort.

Later that night Marie realized that her bed spread and sheets smelled of cat urine. She tore the bed clothes from the bed and threw them in the washing machine. She yelled at Ziggy for almost two full minutes. The next day she made sure the bedroom door was shut when she went to work. If that cat was going to get back at her that way, she at least could keep him out of the room.

Ziggy went back to using the rugs as his litter box. On rare occasions, when Marie lapsed and left the door open, Ziggy would return to his favorite target—the bed. The one place he was not going to return to was his litter box. Since his pain had disappeared by leaving the box alone, he would never voluntarily go back to it.

The interplay between physical maladies and behavioral changes is a normal phenomenon. When an animal's behavior shifts rapidly, the first thing to consider is a medical cause for the change. In Ziggy's case, the initial aversion to the box was caused by a painful infection. Even though the infection subsided, his aversion to the box had remained. The pain had reinforced his behavior.

To get back in touch with her cat, Marie needs to focus on a more basic view of his personality. A medical check up followed by a few day's confinement with a clean box will be a good first step toward correcting the problem. Positive reinforcement for correctly using the box will eventually reform his bad habit.

Cats are more social when treated as such

There is a rumor going around that cats are aloof, untrainable and solitary creatures. I think the rumor was started by dogs trying to protect their status as "man's best friend." The truth is that cats can be very social, highly trainable and real pests at getting your attention—if you let them.

The common perception of cats as remote and cold creatures, is often the result of a self-fulfilling prophecy. Cats that are not allowed to socialize with humans at an early age may never become good with people. Cats that are born indoors and routinely handled as infants usually become affectionate and loving companions. The only real difference between a "house cat" and "barn cat" is the amount of early contact they have with people.

For owners of well-socialized felines, this is not a revelation. Anyone who attempts to read a newspaper or book in the presence of a truly domesticated cat can attest to this. Within a short time, Felix is going to curl up in the one spot guaranteed to prevent you from paying attention to anything other than him. Whether that means lying in your lap, draping over your head or batting things from your desk makes no difference to the cat. The game is to get your attention at all costs.

One "endearing" cat pastime is night prowling. While dogs and humans are creatures who tend to wake with the dawn and sleep after dusk, cats are primarily night creatures. At two in the morning, a cat is as likely to be fully alert and energetic as her owner is to be asleep and unconscious. The sound of nocturnal meowing and falling objects can become a sore spot between them.

Another common misconception about cat behavior is that they are untrainable. A quick way to disprove this theory is to open a can of cat food with an electric can opener a few times. While dogs steadfastly have to be told three times to "sit" before they respond, cats can learn to come to the sound of a can opener with delightful consistency. The primary reason that cats do not appear trainable is that the traditional way of training has been through the use of force. It is not that cats are stupid. It is that they do not like to be pushed around.

Instead of pushing, shoving and tugging, successful cat trainers use tasty tidbits in exchange for good performance. If this use of food seems like a bribe, think of it as "payment for services rendered." If you vary the reinforcements enough, your cat can also learn to come when called, sit, lie down and rollover on command. Many cats learn to retrieve small objects in exchange for affection and the thrill of the chase—just like a dog.

If tricks and obedience behaviors do not interest you, your cat's ability to learn is still an important asset. It will help him adapt to a variety of environments. Many cats learn to ride comfortably in a car, train or airplane. Some cats will rest comfortably, draped around their owner's shoulders, while enjoying a long walk. Kittens that are taught to accept a collar and leash can learn to enjoy self-propelled walks with their owners.

Though not as varied in their physical shape as dogs, cats come in almost as many varieties. From the 20-pound Maine Coon Cat, to delicate exotics such as the Abyssinian Cat, prospective owners can chose a pet that smacks of the great outdoors, or a Victorian drawing room. Hair length can range from cotton candy-like Persians to the wiry haired Cornish Rex. An interesting purebred called the Scottish Fold is named for its ears, which fold down flat against the head rather than standing up.

For many people, cats represent the perfect pet for city living. They require less attention than dogs, cost less to feed and are easier to house. While training is a necessity of dog ownership, it is a pleasant pastime for dedicated cat lovers, not a mandatory activity. A well-socialized cat is a versatile and affectionate companion who can easily keep you occupied for fifteen years, or more.

Litterboxes: In-house outhouses

If you have ever been to an outdoor event, a construction site or campground, you have probably used a "Porta-potty." While relieving oneself in privacy is socially desirable, many people shun these devices and heed "nature's call" behind the nearest bush. The primary reason that a person would risk embarrassment rather than use one of these 21st century outhouses is simple— they usually stink.

Now that I have conjured up an image that is guaranteed to make you wrinkle your nose, imagine how your cat would feel if forced to use a Porta-potty. In case you are wondering what types of people have miniature Porta-potties in their houses, just look closely at the next litter box you see. While we see them as convenient little "kitty commodes," Felix is more likely to view a litter box as a big plastic "in-house outhouse"—one that usually stinks.

The reason for this difference in perspective is understandable. The typical litter box is about four inches tall and overflowing with a mound of clay litter. The litter usually contains a liberal dose of highly secret "odor crystals" designed to mask the smell of cat poop. The typical owner uses a kitchen scoop to stir up the litter every few days and remove any feces. The litter is dumped when the owner starts to be offended by the odor. This is remarkably similar to the way sanitation companies use chemicals to disguise the smell of Porta-potties. The convenience of the sanitation worker is often more important than the occupant's nose.

Rather than choosing cleanliness as the primary goal, some cat owners have been lured down a different path. In the late 1980s a new variety of litter allowed pet owners to be even more neglectful of the box. This new "clumping" litter is so fine that fluids cause it to stick together in little balls that can be removed with a scoop. The companies that sell this stuff suggest that it is good for a month or more. Many cats disagree as to the effective life of this litter.

Another innovation in cat box technology is the covered litter box. These little miracle boxes have odor filters on top to prevent foul and noxious fumes from offending your nose. That air filter on top of the cover is meant to protect your delicate sensitivities—not provide Felix with fresh air. They also afford the cat a sense of privacy—the same claustrophobic privacy available in a Porta-potty. Some cats decide to forego the privacy of a covered box in order to find a less pungent potty area.

While all of these systems appear perfect from a human perspective, they are far from ideal when viewed by a cat. First, the cat is far closer to the litter than you are. Though you may only smell the faint scent of odor crystals, the cat is getting a far more potent aroma. If you want to really appreciate your cat's box, put your nose about an inch above the litter and breathe deeply. Even with perfectly clean litter the smell of dust and odor control chemicals can be overpowering

The real problem is that the typical box of clay litter is rarely cleaned often enough to satisfy a discriminating cat. Clumping litters are not immune to these same problems. As you scoop the clumps from the box, you will notice that some of them disintegrate. This leaves small fragments of urine-soaked litter in the box. If the litter is not changed on a regular basis, it becomes repulsive to the cat far sooner than it does to the owner.

Litter boxes are a wonderful aid for owners who wish to have an indoor cat. In order to correctly imitate a cat's natural potty habits, it is necessary to obey some important, but simple, rules.

- If your cat has any type of inappropriate elimination, seek veterinary help immediately. If the problem is physical, the cleanliness of the box will not solve the problem.
- The box should be in a quiet place. Noisy kids and badgering dogs can easily drive a cat to the nearest piece of carpet rather than the most immaculate litter box.
- The box must be clean from the standpoint of the cat. This

means occasionally washing it out with a disinfectant such as a mild chlorine bleach solution.

- A good rule of thumb is to use less litter and change it more often. Try covering the box with 1/2 inch of litter. Each time your cat uses it, dump it out.
- Have at least one box per cat. Some cats will not use the box if another cat has eliminated in it. Many finicky cats refuse to urinate and poop in the same box. Two boxes, side by side, can solve this problem.

How the mind and body build new behaviors

Fluffy had a bladder infection. She first noticed it while using her litter box. The act of eliminating had gradually become painful. Fluffy didn't know about bacteria and infections. She thought the pain was caused by the box.

To remedy her discomfort, Fluffy started to experiment. She could not stop eliminating, but she could try new locations. Her first goal was to find a surface that felt like fresh dirt. She raked her paws across a variety of surfaces until she felt the same resistance she got from her cat litter.

Fluffy's first target was the carpet in the dining room. It was as far from the box as she could get. The tight nap of the carpet gave the same sensation to her paws as her litter. She sniffed to see if the spot was clean and then eliminated. Fluffy got a rude surprise—it still hurt.

The second location she tried was the bed in the guest bedroom. The ribbed comforter had the proper feeling as she pulled her claws across it. The surface moved a little bit as she pulled at it, just like litter. Fluffy eliminated on the comforter. She was again frustrated in her attempts. Her infection was still causing pain.

After several weeks, Fluffy's owner started to smell a peculiar odor in the house. The inescapable conclusion was that Fluffy was wetting on the carpet.

A quick trip to the vet confirmed the suspicion. Fluffy got lots of antibiotics and would soon be well. Her owner was relieved to know that Fluffy's behavior was caused by a physical problem. Everything would get back to normal once the medication did its job.

After her visit to the vet, Fluffy used the box again. Antibiotics take a few days to start working so the return to the box was painful. Fluffy was further convinced that the box caused the pain. She continued her quest to find a painless place to eliminate.

As the medication started to take effect, Fluffy's discomfort decreased. This confirmed that she could reduce the pain by avoiding the box. By this point, Fluffy was one step away from never using the box again.

To get Fluffy back on track, several things must happen. First, she must be prevented from having more accidents in the house. Second, she must be forced to use her box, and third, she must be reinforced for correct elimination.

The easiest way to prevent more accidents is to confine her to a room with a slick floor. Fluffy has an instinctive preference for surfaces that can be moved around. A concrete or tile floor is less likely to stimulate elimination than carpet. Fluffy is going to spend a few days in the laundry room.

The slick surface leaves Fluffy with only one suitable area to eliminate—her box. The first time she is forced to use it she will anticipate the pain that she experienced before. She may try to avoid urinating as long as she can. When she finally eliminates she will be pleasantly surprised—no more pain. If her owner is smart, Fluffy will spend about a week in the laundry room. Whenever her owner hears her using the box, Fluffy is going to receive lots of praise and food treats. She is going to learn that using the box is a pleasant experience.

It is obvious that pain and discomfort from an illness can change the behavior of a normally perfect pet. It is important to remember that relieving the physical cause of the problem may not automatically correct the behavior. Getting Fluffy to return to the box will require a combination of medical and behavioral solutions.

Part 4:
Care and Keeping

Every-puppy out of the pool

One of the many enjoyable activities of summer is swimming. While we send our children to swimming classes and hire lifeguards to watch over us, few pet owners extend this concern to their pets.

Those dogs that readily take to water are trusted immediately, while non-swimmers are barred from the pool for life. Ironically, it is the non-swimmer that needs to know about water safety most. Even a dog that is not allowed in the pool may still accidentally end up in the water. Fortunately, teaching canine water safety only requires that you teach one behavior—getting out of the pool.

If you can swim, you have already learned, and solved, one of the problems that dogs have when swimming—how to get air. If you watch a dog's posture you will note that to swim, a dog holds his nose out of the water and paddles vigorously with his legs. Looking closely you will notice that his eyes are positioned well behind his nose. As the dog's head rocks backward to prevent water from flowing into his nose, the dog is actually looking upward, at an angle. This is the equivalent view that you would have if you were floating on your back, being towed by your feet.

While swimming with his head aimed upward, the dog's vision is limited. Rather than looking straight ahead, he is seeing the roof of your house and the sky. His peripheral vision can help to compensate for this, but because his nose blocks his vision to the front, he can't see anything directly ahead or under the water. If a dog accidentally falls into the pool, he must swim until his foot hits something solid, because he has no idea where the pool steps are. The decorative tile on the edge of the pool gives no clue about how to escape. Successfully escaping is usually a matter of luck.

Long-coated dogs have an additional problem if they fall into the pool. As their coats get soaked, it becomes harder to move through the water. Imagine swimming in the ocean while wearing a mink coat. The dog soon tires and his hind quarters start to sink lower in the water. Now the dog is merely concerned with keeping his nose above water. He has no way to hold his breath and float as a human might. Exhaustion quickly leads to drowning.

The first step to protecting your dog is to identify the way out of the pool. Since the dog is looking up while swimming, you must place a readily observable object high enough to be visible to the dog. Get in the pool and swim with your eyes just above the water. Select a point that is observable from any spot in the pool that always leads to the steps. Use this spot to orient your dog to the escape route.

Once you have selected your exit point you must choose a suitable landmark to guide your dog. Dogs primarily see in shades of gray rather than in color. You should pick something that incorporates highly contrasting tones such as black and white, rather than colored objects. If your pool has a fence, you can candy stripe a vertical part of the fence with contrasting tape. Select the one bar that can be seen from all points in the pool, or a section of the top rail of the fence. Another alternative would be a bamboo pole, striped with black tape and mounted vertically in the ground or secured to the fence. For decorative purposes you might add a whirligig or a windsock. Dogs see movement very well, even in dim light.

The next step is to place the dog in the pool. Attach a long lightweight rope to his collar to pull him out in case of an emergency. Leave enough slack to allow him free movement. Start with the dog one body length away from the exit point. As the dog is released, call to him. When his foot touches the step, continue coaxing until he gets completely out of the water. Give him special treats, praise and affection for successfully exiting the pool. Gradually increase the distance that he must go to find the steps. When Bowser can escape the pool from any point, reduce your involvement by leaving the pool area completely after releasing him into the water. His only guide to safety will be the visual aids you have placed near the steps. Watch very carefully from a hiding place and be prepared to get him out quickly at the first signs of difficulty.

If you are working with a puppy, be cautious about over-extending the workout. Puppies tire suddenly. If his hind quarters start to sink lower in the water, be prepared to jump in and get him or pull him out with a rope. Try not to traumatize him, but get him out quickly. Repeat this routine until Bowser can find the escape route from anywhere in the pool.

Water safety is an often overlooked part of our dogs' training. Regardless of whether or not your dog is allowed in the pool, you should make the effort to teach him to get out of one. For information regarding CPR for pet owners, contact your veterinarian or your local Veterinary Medical Association.

How to teach your pet to say AAHHHHHH!!!!

At the Brookfield Zoo in Chicago there is a diabetic orangutan who must give blood samples, and take insulin injections every day. While it is not a new phenomenon for zoo animals to be poked and prodded by veterinarians, this orangutan is remarkable for two reasons—he participates in these medical procedures voluntarily and he was taught to do so.

A major problem for veterinarians, groomers and pet owners is to get animals to passively accept necessary pain and discomfort. Many animals are unintentionally yet systematically taught to hate veterinarians because the only time they experience physical discomfort is when they are in the clinic. Matted little Lhasa Apsos tend to bite the hands that groom them because they object to having their hair pulled for long periods of time. Many pet owners are bitten while attempting to trim their pet's nails, as a result of poor handling technique.

Over the years, methods of physically restraining animals have become safer for the handlers and diabolical for the animals. Fractious horses are usually restrained with a device called a "twitch." This gizmo looks like a pair of crab-cracking pliers that are closed down on the horse's upper lip. If your upper lip is in this type of hand-held vise, you are going to stand very still while you are being poked, prodded or vaccinated. Dogs are often prevented from biting with leather or nylon fabric muzzles, while cats may be placed in canvas bags that expose only the part of the animal to be examined.

In contrast to the traditional forms of restraint, marine mammal trainers have long taught "husbandry" behaviors to their animals to facilitate medical exams and treatment.

Dolphins, whales, otters and sea lions are routinely taught to slip out of the water and give urine samples, blood samples and accept injections, on command.

For the pet owner, teaching husbandry behaviors can help a pet become accustomed to necessary handling. Teaching a dog or cat to stand quietly while being examined or to be still while having his nails trimmed is not a difficult task. The benefit to the animal is obvious. If you would like to teach your pet these types of behavior, here are some simple suggestions to get started.

- Occasionally board your pet at a veterinary clinic when he is healthy, to get him used to the sights, sounds and smell of a clinic. If the only time he goes there is when he is treated, staying overnight can become traumatic in itself.

- Handle your pet's feet on a regular basis. Gently and firmly hold the animal's paw for one or two seconds. Give a treat or affection for passive behavior. At first, limit the handling to brief moments of success and gradually extend the length of time you can manipulate the paw. If you are going to use clippers to trim the pet's nails, start by merely touching the trimmers to the nail and giving the animal a treat. Then squeeze the trimmer gently around the nail and release the pressure. Do not actually trim the nail until after the pet is completely comfortable with this process. If you aren't sure how to trim the nail, ask your veterinarian to demonstrate the correct technique. Resist the temptation to grip the dog tighter to prevent escape. The idea is to make this a pleasurable experience.

- To teach your pet to be groomed, grip the animal's hair in your fingers and pull gently. Give treats and affection periodically if the animal remains quiet. Do not expect the pet to remain for long periods of time on the first few sessions. Gradually build the amount of time you can tug the pet's hair before you switch to a real brush or comb.

- Teaching a puppy or kitten to accept handling is far easier than teaching an adult. Try to start the training when the animal is old enough to come to your home. Plan for those experiences that you know will be important to an adult animal and start planning early.

- To teach Fido or Felix to accept injections, pinch the skin lightly at the base of the animal's neck and give a treat. Gradually increase the pressure a little until the feeling of getting pinched is strongly associated with the treat that follows.
- Ask your vet or groomer if you can come to their business and sit in the waiting room at times other than when actual treatment or grooming is to take place. If Fido goes to the doctor many times but only gets shots once in a while, he is more likely to enjoy trips to the vet.
- Handle your pet's mouth often. Lift the lips and look at the teeth and gums. Get the animal used to having human fingers touching teeth, tongue and gums on a regular basis.
- Watch a veterinary exam and notice how the veterinarian feels a pet's abdomen, paws and head. Learn how to flex your pet's limbs to move them through their natural range of movement. Try to recreate these manipulations at home where the pet is more comfortable.

Premium food or premium prices

Q: What's the difference between a Hartz Jerky Chew'm dog treat and Romanoff Black Lumpfish Caviar?

A: The caviar is cheaper per pound—by a wide margin.

On a recent tour of my local supermarket I stopped by the pet food aisle. I had just bought some Hill's Science Diet cat food from my veterinarian. It was more than $2 per pound or about 12 cents per ounce. Everybody knows that those fancy foods like Science Diet and Iams are just puffed up yuppie status symbols. Only an idiot would spend $20 for a 10-pound bag of cat food, right? Guess again.

One of the least known facts about pet food is the actual cost of various brands. The same person who would scoff at my 12 cents-an-ounce Science Diet may turn around and buy a box of Tender Vittles dry cat food at the local supermarket. The price per ounce—12 cents. The premium food is exactly the same price as the name brand diet.

This comparison between brands is even more complex than the price would indicate. Price is not always a good indicator of the nutritional value of pet food. The real test is how much of the food your animal can digest and use as nutrients.

For instance, a national brand dog food is $16 for 40 pounds. The premium food is $18 for 20 pounds. The national brand looks like a bargain until you notice that Rover sure does need to go outside a lot lately. Your savings were mostly indigestible filler that passed right through the dog and ended up on your lawn. By contrast, the premium food has less filler and more digestible nutrients. A higher proportion of nutrients goes to the dog and less of the filler fertilizes your grass.

Making an evaluation and comparison between pet foods is not easy. Even discovering the exact contents of the food is a confusing journey. The Food and Drug Administration requires that ingredients be listed on pet food packages. The list starts with the ingredient that forms the largest part of the item and then works downward. If the list says water, cornmeal, rocks, it means that the item is mostly water, with less cornmeal than water, and less rocks than corn meal. This seems like a straightforward approach until you realize that the label on the front of the package may have little to do with the required ingredients label.

King Kuts, a brand of canned dog food, bears the words "with real beef" on one of its varieties, and "with real beef and liver" on another. On the back, the ingredients tell another story. The primary ingredient is "water, sufficient for processing." The next ingredient listed is not beef, but chicken. Beef is actually the fifth ingredient listed.

Skippy brand "Burgers and Cheese" for dogs, has a similar label. The image of hamburger patties and cheese helps to sell the product. The primary ingredient? You guessed it, "water, sufficient for processing." Meat byproducts are No. 3, after soy flour. The cheese is listed as a distant 13th. It appears that Skippy believes that "Burgers and Cheese" sounds more appetizing than "Water and Soy Flour Flavored."

Cat food also suffers from this marketing mayhem. Purina Tender Vittles Tuna Flavor is primarily "water, sufficient for processing." The next items listed are poultry byproducts, meal, corn gluten meal, and in 11th place, tuna meal. Friskies for Cats Ocean Fish Flavor is mostly ground yellow corn. The next ingredient is poultry, followed by something called "digest." Digest is described as "poultry byproducts, fish and fish byproducts—source of ocean fish flavor." This is like describing a new Ford truck as being "rubberlike" because it has tires. The ironic part of this is that the real ingredients do not always cost as much per pound as some of the fillers and substitutes.

Shopping for pet food and treats can be a perplexing business. The labels are confusing, the claims are misleading and the nutritional values of some foods are dubious. Finding a proper food for your pet should be the result of your own research and consultations with your veterinarian regarding the nutritional needs of your pet.

The dangers of urban living

A woman in Florida was keeping a friend's dog for a few days. The dog was scheduled to be adopted by a new owner. The day before the dog was to go to its new home, the woman found the dog dead. The dog had been left in the yard, wearing a choke chain. This type of collar is also called a slip or training collar. They are usually metal, but may also be made of braided cloth or nylon. When the end of the chain is pulled, it constricts around the dog's neck. The dog had attempted to dig her way under a chain link fence. Half way under the fence she tried to back out again. The ring on her collar caught on the fence. As she struggled frantically to escape, she choked to death. As tragic as that death was, the choke chain was not the real culprit. The actual killers were ignorance and complaisance.

Another behavior that risks tragedy is allowing a dog to ride in the bed of a pickup truck. Often the owner's logic suggests that since the dog has never fallen out of the truck, it never will. This logic falls apart when one realizes that a flat tire, a quick stop or a minor accident could eject Fido from the truck.

One of the most obvious killer behaviors is allowing a dog to run free in the city. The notion that a dog can be "street-wise" is very common. The actual ability of a dog to avoid injury on the street is limited. Rather than developing the ability to watch out for cars, the opposite occurs. When Rover sees his first car approaching, he is likely to hear the brakes squeal and see it stop. If the car does not actually hit him, he will soon develop a disdain for those important cues. The bad news for Rover is that someday a motorist is not going to be able to stop.

A consideration that few pet owners appreciate is that the death of their pet is not the only consequence of running loose.

A traffic accident caused by an animal running in traffic or falling from a vehicle is the responsibility of the owner. While still on the topic of automobiles, I should mention automobile antifreeze. According to experts, antifreeze tastes sweet. Dogs and cats love and will seek out the fluorescent green liquid. Even a few ounces can kill a large dog. During fall and spring, motorists often drain their radiators or have excess coolant boil out onto the ground. This is a real danger for any pets in the area.

These are just a few of the obviously hazardous situations that may confront your pet. The days of living on a farm without leashes, collars or traffic are over. The additional price of urban pet ownership is an awareness of our pets' helplessness in a complex society. To really care for them requires more than food, water and shelter—it takes forethought.

Home health exams— and an ounce of prevention

About three weeks ago I was rubbing my dog's chest when I noticed a lump under the skin. Megan is a very healthy dog, but she is ten years old and has a history of benign tumors. Our veterinarian performed a biopsy of the lump and recorded its size and location. If the lump grows, we can measure against our early examination and be able to determine the rate of growth.

One of the greatest gifts you can give your pet is a routine examination. Domesticated pets may experience pain for weeks or months without displaying outward signs of discomfort. Since your pet cannot communicate directly, you must learn to watch for signs of disease and injury.

A good place to start your exam is with your animal's head. Your animal's eyes should be bright and clear. Older pets may have a blue-gray haze that is a natural part of aging. Some dogs have a condition called entropion where the eye lids roll inward. The lashes scratch the cornea and can cause impaired vision and ultimately blindness. Make sure the lashes look like yours and point away from the eye.

Ears can be a source of infection for many animals. Cats and dogs whose ears stand up often collect dust and debris as well as parasites such as ear mites. Dogs whose ears flop have their own brand of problems. The ear lies flat against the head like the front flap of a purse. While this prevents debris and dust from entering, it traps in moisture and heat—a veritable Disneyland for microorganisms. When you examine your dog's ear, try to look as far down into the canal as possible. If you see very dark "dirt" deep within the ear, your pet may be infested with ear mites. A trip to the vet is warranted whenever you suspect foreign debris in your pet's ears.

The mouth is the next logical area to investigate in your home exam. Instead of a visual exam at first, try your nose. Open your pet's mouth gently with your fingers. Place your nose close to the pet's mouth and breath in through your nose. A foul odor usually means dental neglect or some other problem.

Your next observation is a visual check of the gums and teeth. Gums should be firm and pink. Press a spot on the gums and watch it closely. It should turn white as your pressure forces blood to recede. As you take your finger away the rosy pink color should quickly return.

The pet's teeth should be held to the same standards as your own. Dark tartar and stains are signs of neglect. Broken or chipped teeth can be a source of general infection that could lead to serious medical problems.

Moving from the head, it is a good idea to examine the animal's forelegs, neck and shoulders. Ticks and fleas can infest your animal without your knowledge in a very short time. Flea colonies usually are accompanied by small scabby areas. Ticks swell as they engorge themselves on the animal's blood. They appear as a small flexible sack about the size of a pea. This is also a good time to examine for lumps and tumors.

Pass your hands across the rest of the dog's body. Look for abrasions, cuts and bumps. In most cases, the pet's coat should be shiny. Mats and tangles that do not show up visually are best found during this type of examination. Pay close attention to the pet's paws, toes and nails, as well as the rectal area. If your animal will allow it, roll it on its back and look at the chest, belly and groin areas too.

In general, routine examinations can help to further your pet's health. Injuries and diseases are invariably best treated when they are detected. To accentuate your ability to do this, ask your veterinarian to help you develop a regular diagnostic checkup that you can perform. If your pet will not allow you to touch it in this fashion, you may need to teach the animal to stay still while being examined. The time and effort you spend teaching this behavior could save your pet's life.

Using a crate: Greater freedom comes from gentle confinement

What do you do if you want to have your dog indoors, but he is not fully house trained? How can you trust that your new pet won't tear up the carpet or eat the sofa when you go to work? Unless you don't work, have lots of spare time to supervise a pooch and enough money for a private trainer, you may be in trouble. The obvious solution is to have a safe and comfortable area for your pet that is immune to destruction and improper elimination. Many pet owners are using airline carriers or cages to solve this problem.

Professional trainers, handlers and hunters have used crates and cages as a matter of course for many years. Large dog and cat shows would be unmanageable without the convenience and safety of proper confinement. Wise hunters prefer to secure their dogs in a crate rather than letting them bounce around the back of an open pickup truck.

While animal-care professionals and hobbyists universally approve of crates and cages, some pet owners still believe that a crate somehow harms the animal's psyche. In reality, dogs and cats are notorious for curling up for many hours at a time in small, dark, quiet spaces. A little positive reinforcement for entering and remaining in the crate can go a long way toward making necessary confinement a pleasant experience.

One of the best uses for a crate is to create an "accident-free zone" for your puppy. When you cannot watch the pup closely, confinement in a crate allows you to be sure that the animal has not eliminated. When you do take the pup outside you can be sure that it will need to eliminate and you can be prepared to positively reinforce the correct behavior. A crate can also prevent your puppy from chewing on inappropriate items while you are sleeping or otherwise occupied.

The amount of time you may keep an animal in a crate each day should be determined by what you are trying to achieve. An average of eight hours per day can be safely maintained almost indefinitely.

Longer periods of confinement can cause problems. Consistently requiring a dog to hold its fluids for ten or more hours daily can lead to bladder infections and other disorders. Another danger of long periods of confinement is that the animal may eliminate out of desperation. Once the animal has lost its inhibition against soiling the crate, it is very difficult to correct the problem.

Crates and cages come in a variety of forms. Aluminum flight kennels can resist almost any type of abuse but tend to be hot in warm weather. Heavy wire cages add the comfort of available breezes but may tend to rust in wet climates and do not afford protection from the elements. A compromise between these two extremes is the hard plastic kennel that is fitted with a heavy wire door. These plastic crates have become the industry standard. An additional benefit to enclosed crates of metal or plastic is that they may be stacked on top of each other while traveling, at a dog show, or at home. Another advantage of plastic crates is that they can be easily disassembled for storage. The top and bottom halves of the crate fit inside each other to form a compact shell. They are also easy to clean and sterilize.

Prices range from $10.00 for an inexpensive cat carrier to over $500.00 for an aluminum carrier big enough for a St. Bernard. Plastic crates for medium to large dogs range from about $25.00 to $125.00 for the largest sizes. Crates are available through pet shops, variety stores, wholesale catalogs and at dog or cat shows.

- Start your animal early. If the animal is exposed to the crate as an infant, you will have much less trouble confining the adult animal.
- Start with short periods of confinement and then gradually increase the amount of time the animal must remain in the crate.

- Make sure the crate is big enough—but not too big. Measure the animal from the base of the skull to the base of the tail. The crate must be at least as long as this measurement. The animal's height should be measured from the top of its shoulders to the ground. It is acceptable for the dog to stoop a little to get into the crate. If you have a puppy, ask your veterinarian to help you estimate the adult size of your pet.

- If you have a doggie door, you can use the crate to speed the process of house training. First, remove the door from the crate. Secure the crate against the inside of the doggie door. Now Fido can remain in the crate for shelter or go outside to eliminate.

- A crate is an ideal tool for traveling. Many hotels and motels will allow pets that are crate-trained. It also allows you to secure the animal in case of an unexpected breakdown or other emergency.

A dark but common tale

The evening air was hot and muggy by the freshly irrigated cornfield south of Chandler, Arizona. A beat-up, mid-70s Pontiac sedan pulled over quickly on the gravel shoulder. Amid hushed and hurried voices, the rear door was opened and something was shoved out. The car spewed gravel from its rear tires as it roared away. A very confused puppy dodged the gravel and scampered into the stand of corn.

Buster was only four months old. His whole life had been spent in houses and yards. He had no way of knowing why he was abandoned in this curious place. In fact he didn't yet realize that he was alone.

Buster peered from behind the corn stalks and watched the car disappear down the road. An involuntary whine escaped from his throat. He scampered quickly after the car. The I.D. tags that usually jingled from his collar as he walked were curiously silent. The Family had removed any chance of tracing Buster back to them. Being alone was nothing new to Buster. He had been left alone many times before, but always in the walled backyard of the Family. This new place frightened him and caused him to whimper. He trotted aimlessly in the direction of the Pontiac—and the Family.

Back in the car, the woman gripped the steering wheel tightly. She glanced furtively in the rear view mirror and saw headlights behind her. Her daughter had almost botched it trying to get the tags off the collar. The woman was afraid someone had seen them. As she scanned the mirror, her eyes caught a glimpse of a small silhouette in the roadway behind her—it was Buster. Her heart twinged for a moment and then hardened. The Man had said that either she got rid of the dog, or he would leave her. She could not let that happen. She had two kids. She had no job. Even the car was his.

The daughter started asking the woman about Buster's future. She wondered if he would be found by a good family and live on a farm. She asked if he would have plenty to eat and a soft bed to sleep on. The Woman told the girl to shut up and smacked her across the head. She was afraid of the girl's questions because she might be tempted to answer them truthfully.

As Buster wandered down the center of the road, he was so focused on the Pontiac that he didn't hear the pickup truck behind him. The driver was fiddling with his car radio and barely saw the pup in time to swerve. Buster looked at the headlights of the truck and froze. The driver muttered something about stupid farm people who let their dogs run loose. It never dawned on him that this pup was the victim of more than rural folk ways.

As the truck flashed past him, Buster's paralysis turned into panic-stricken flight. He darted toward the opposite side of the road. He landed on the far bank of an irrigation ditch and fell backward into the water. This he knew how to handle.

The Family owned a swimming pool. Buster had fallen in several times and had become adept at scrambling out of the cool water. This was similar, yet somehow different.

In the pool, the way out was always stationary. This funny little pool was moving. As he tried to scramble up the sloped edge of the ditch, the water swept his hind legs farther down stream. He failed several times before he finally heaved himself out of the water. He collapsed in the dirt and fell asleep.

When he woke up, he saw some lights in the distance. He knew what lights were, but these were much farther away than any he had seen before. He trotted wearily toward the lights until he came to a house. He hoped he would find the Family there.

Buster approached the house slowly. Rascal, the farm dog, smelled Buster's scent on the breeze and moved toward the puppy. Rascal was a seasoned veteran of countless skirmishes with coyotes and stray dogs. He raced toward Buster and slammed into him at full speed.

Buster was too young and too exhausted to fight. He turned away from the bigger dog and struggled to escape. Rascal's teeth nipped his neck and shoulders. Buster screamed and ran into the night, tail between his legs. He ran until he could barely stand and sank to the ground under a bush. He was completely alone.

Buster's story is not unusual. Despite accepted alternatives, many people choose to abandon an animal rather than make the tough decisions that often accompany pet ownership. The real solution to this problem is simple. If you cannot care for your animal, let someone else do it. If you are unable to find a good home for your pet, let a humane group relieve you of the responsibility.

Though not all sheltered animals are adopted, it is far better for them to be humanely destroyed than dumped on a deserted stretch of road. Abandoned animals rarely survive for long. They succumb to hazards such as automobiles, wild animals, disease, harsh weather and starvation. Their deaths are rarely peaceful.

As for Buster, his fate is not known. Perhaps he was adopted by that farm family, or perhaps not. He was last seen trotting down the road—following a car that looked vaguely like a Pontiac.

Pets can share with the disabled

In the late 1960s I visited a small swim-suit shop in La Jolla, California. As I entered, I was greeted by a large German Shepherd Dog with snow-white eyes. The dog was obviously blind. Just as I made a million assumptions about the "poor disabled dog," a small Shetland Sheep Dog trotted up and wiggled her fanny under the Shepherd's nose. The larger dog automatically lowered his head onto the dog's back and both dogs walked briskly into the adjoining park a short distance away. The Sheltie was guiding the Shepherd.

While the special relationship between these two dogs probably developed naturally, the ability of dogs to lend their senses to humans is a well-established byproduct of domestication. At its most basic level, a dog's abilities to herd, hunt, protect or track are all examples of this canine cooperation. Each of these tasks can be performed better by the dog than by the human because of its superior senses, agility, speed or stamina. There is fundamentally no difference between a dog using its sense of smell to aid a hunter and using its exceptional hearing, eyesight and sense of smell to guard a flock of sheep.

Once you have accepted that dogs can do simple behaviors, it is a small step to teach dogs to do more complex tasks. The ancient use of dogs to attack intruders and enemies was refined during World War I to include reconnaissance and message carrying. After the war, the widespread use of chlorine gas had rendered many veterans blind. Former German army dog handlers turned their talents to developing the first "seeing-eye" dogs. Guide dogs soon came into usage in other countries.

After almost 70 years of work as "seeing eyes," dogs are now used in many other fields of service. For the last 20 years, the use of dogs to assist hearing-impaired humans has progressed from an oddity to an established practice. "Hearing dogs" usually are trained to inform the owner of such everyday sounds as smoke alarms, doorbells, alarm clocks and telephones. Hearing dogs are taught unique behaviors that are associated with specific sounds. The correct response to a knock on the door would be to alert the owner and then take them to the source of the sound. In the event of a fire, the procedure is reversed. The sound of a smoke alarm must cause the dog to guide the owner to an exit away from the fire.

A more ambitious trend in training assistance animals has been in the area of help for the severely disabled. Canine Companions for Independence (CCI), based in Santa Rosa, California, provides dogs for people with a variety of needs. Rather than sticking to "seeing eye" and "hearing ear" dogs, CCI dogs are often trained to assist paraplegics and quadriplegics. These dogs perform vital tasks that require consistency, skill and judgment. For someone confined to a wheelchair, simple acts such as handing money to a sales clerk or turning on a light switch can require great effort. A trained dog can remove much of the frustration associated with mundane tasks as well as developing a deep emotional bond with his master.

While acceptance of assistance dogs has increased dramatically, their numbers are growing at a modest rate. Recent legislation, such as the Americans with Disabilities Act (ADA), affords any certified assistance animal the same access to public accommodations and transportation formerly reserved for guide dogs. With such general approval, the greatest limitations to the use of service dogs are the amount of time and money needed to raise and train one. While the initial cost of the animal is usually nominal, the bulk of the expense is due to the many hours of training necessary to create a dependable working dog.

Because of the investment involved, selecting an animal is usually an important part of the process. The dogs must be enthusiastic but controllable. For instance, a dog that is trained to pull a wheel chair must not pull the person from the chair. A dog trained to help a person undress must not accidentally remove skin along with the socks. Even the job of taking a loaf of bread from a shelf requires great control—the dog must grab the bread without crushing the bread or puncturing the plastic wrapper.

As groups like CCI broaden the traditional roles of service dogs, new applications are being developed for their skills. Dogs have been trained to perform exotic behaviors such as giving warning to epileptics of an impending seizure and more mundane uses such as detecting termites. In a world that favors technological solutions, it is comforting to know that "man's best friend" is not obsolete. After 10,000 years of faithful service, it looks as if dogs will be valued members of society for a long, long time.

Dog catching for amateurs

Yesterday, I saw a small dog run across the street in front of my car. The dog was running toward a woman who was walking her Poodle. As the woman recognized the danger to the beast, she frantically tried to call the dog to her—an unnecessary gesture—the dog made a bee line toward the Poodle. As the woman bent over to grab his collar, the dog ungratefully bit her hand and darted back into the street. He was last seen running off at top speed down the middle of the road.

It is not uncommon for people to attempt to help a lost animal. Animal control agencies will never have enough personnel to be able to control every loose animal. When well-meaning citizens attempt to handle these situations, they may actually do more damage than good. By sharpening your dog-catching skills you may be better prepared to resolve this common problem.

A word of caution before you embark on your quest to save that stray kitty or puppy. Animal control personnel are trained to safely capture and handle lost, frightened and injured pets—you are not. If you cause an accident by chasing an animal into a busy street, you may be liable for any injuries or damages. You may also be injured or killed in the process. When in doubt, call the appropriate agency to handle the problem.

- The first rule of dog catching is not to get hit by a car. It is extremely easy to allow the animal's peril to cloud your judgment. Your humanitarian goal will not stop a car from hitting you. While you may get an award for sacrificing your life to save a pet, it has one serious drawback—it is posthumous.
- Place yourself between the animal and a dangerous situation. If the dog is headed toward a busy intersection, you may startle

the dog by sneaking up behind it. Without appearing to be interested in the animal, go beyond it and attempt to slow or stop its progress before it gets to the intersection. If your presence does spook the animal, it will run away from you and the danger.

- Towering over a dog is perceived by the animal as a threat. Squat or sit on the ground to make the animal feel less threatened.
- Do not make direct eye contact. Dogs perceive staring as a challenge. Look at the dog from the corner of your eye.
- As the dog approaches, offer your hand under the dog's mouth and nose and allow the animal to make the first move. Touching a dog on top of the head, neck or shoulders may trigger a bite or cause the animal to run away.
- Keep a pair of long, soft shoelaces in your car for emergencies. One lace can be used as a makeshift leash while the other can be used to muzzle an injured dog. Ask your veterinarian to show you how to restrain an injured animal.
- A blanket is a great tool for controlling an injured critter. By covering the animal's head or body you can calm the animal down while limiting its ability to hurt you.
- Secure the animal at your home, or a safe place. If you need assistance catching or confining the animal, call your local animal control or police department. Do not be surprised if they cannot offer you immediate help—they are usually swamped with calls.
- It is unfair to expect a veterinarian to perform free treatment for an injured animal. If you wish to be a humanitarian you must accept the financial responsibility.

Pet psychics? I think not!

A few weeks ago I watched a network program that featured a look at our attitudes toward animals. One of the people interviewed was a woman who claimed to have psychic communication with pets. She told one man that his dog wanted to know if his new girlfriend was going to be hanging around for a long time. She also claimed to read the mind of a lizard whose eyes could rotate independently of each other.

It is an appealing idea to believe that we can talk directly to animals. Many people give money to self-proclaimed experts who claim that they can communicate directly with their pets. Some of these experts even make recommendations regarding the medical condition of the animal. Since the person's alleged ability appears to defy observation, it is usually left unchallenged. If you find this type of thing appalling and need some ammunition, here are a few logical questions that should be asked before you swallow it—hook, line and sinker.

Imagine that you are standing on some railroad tracks looking off into the distance. The tracks appear to converge until they come together on the horizon. Now imagine looking behind you and seeing the other end of the tracks meet at the other horizon. Now try to see the tracks disappear to both horizons at the same time. As your eyes cross and your scalp begins to overheat, you realize that you simply can't do it. Ahhh, but a lizard can! Many lizards have eyes that can rotate so that one eye looks forward while the other looks back. So, if a human could actually read the images from a lizard's mind, two questions arise. First, how could that person possibly look in two opposite directions at once, and second, if you did experience it, wouldn't you mention such a bizarre sensation?

Was the Cocker Spaniel nervous about whether a man's new girl friend was going to be hanging around for a while? This seems pretty straightforward on the surface. Why couldn't a dog wonder about such a thing? Because it requires that dogs possess an ability that is truly beyond them—the ability to imagine events in the future.

Dogs do not understand time as humans do. They are creatures of the moment in everything they do. A dog will turn over his water bowl in 100-degree heat with no other source for water, with no thought for his future thirst. Canines cannot imagine five minutes from now, or even five seconds. The only way a dog can relate to the future is when a prelearned chain of events happens. That is how they anticipate the time that you get home from work each day, or that you put your jogging shoes on just before you take Fido for a walk. They do not worry about next Tuesday. To test this assertion, ask your dog to sit—tomorrow. Suddenly Fido doesn't seem quite so easy to understand. He certainly knows how to sit, but how can you communicate to him that it should be done in the future? Our psychic friend can't explain that either, yet she claims that the Cocker is concerned about the longevity of the new girlfriend.

It is very easy to claim to have special powers of communication with animals. It can also be very lucrative. The problem with this practice is that it fosters an image of animals that is nothing more than a cartoon caricature of their real existence. The gullibility of sincere animal lovers places these pretenders in positions of undeserved authority. To accept a psychic's opinion about the medical and behavioral treatment of a pet is risky business.

Konrad Lorenz, the famed ethologist once said that speculations of this type "... are pure inventions, or at best, self-deceptions of uncritical observers. Yet, as is so often the case, the truth about an animal is far more exciting and altogether more beautiful than all the myths woven about it." With all of the obvious differences between pets and people, it is ironic that some humans want to believe that pets are actually little carbon copies of ourselves. Before you get caught up in listening to canine channelers and feline phrenologists, pretend you are a lizard who can look in two directions at once—and take a second look at them.

Neutering/spaying boosts health, lifespan of animals

Mark and Betty have a little mutt named Doogie. Doogie is about three years old and has a wonderful life. Every day he sneaks around the house and sprinkles urine on the drapes and furniture. When guests come, he invariably gets amorous with the guest's leg or with one of Mark and Betty's children. Each evening he gets to wander the neighborhood and mark his outdoor territory. Sometimes he gets to mate with a female dog, and sometimes he gets into a fight. Doogie also eats the neighbor's garbage and plays "dodge the bumper" with fast-moving cars. In case you haven't guessed, Doogie isn't neutered.

One of the reasons Doogie isn't neutered is because Mark doesn't believe in it. When anyone mentions neutering, he asks them how they would like to be "fixed." "Besides, when a dog gets fixed," Mark says, "it gets fat and lazy." That usually silences the critics.

Mark has had many dogs in his adult life and so far none of them have been neutered. None of them have died of old age, either.

In this day of pet overpopulation, it seems strange that people still resist sterilizing their pets. Even more surprising is that the objections are rarely based in fact, but rather in myth and ignorance.

One such myth is that allowing a female dog to have at least one litter improves her personality. This belief is held despite the common knowledge that female dogs are notorious for biting people in defense of their pups. Once the dog learns this type of aggression, it does not automatically go away after the pups are weaned. Having one litter may actually increase irritability and aggression rather than reducing it. Also, clinical studies indicate that spaying a dog before her first heat cycle is an almost perfect insurance against breast cancer.

Another commonly held notion is that altered pets gain weight and get lethargic. One effect of spaying and neutering is that the animal's metabolism slows down slightly. The weight gain results from the simple process of overfeeding. The truth is that animals do not get fat and lazy because of neutering, but from overeating and underexercising.

Opponents of spaying and neutering are not the only ones who stretch or obscure the truth. It is assumed by many pet fanciers that sterilization is a cure for all types of aggression, scent-marking, mounting behavior and hyperactivity. These statements are overly simplistic exaggerations. Scientific studies indicate that sterilization does not affect all animals equally.

Aggression between males is a common problem for dog and cat owners. Neutering will affect about 60 percent of dogs and 90 percent of cats. In general, the problem of "mounting" behavior holds to this proportion as well. Roaming behavior is reduced the most—about 90 percent in both dogs and cats. Scent-marking shows an even wider difference, with 90 percent of cats decreasing the behavior while only 50 percent of dogs are affected.

Even though sterilization is not a cure-all, it can have medical and behavioral benefits for your cat or dog. Here are some spay/neuter facts to help you make an informed decision:

- Sterilization can reduce or prevent certain types of cancer, or other medical problems. Early neutering does prevent testicular cancer, a common problem in dogs. Female dogs who are spayed before puberty are effectively immune to breast cancer. Check with your veterinarian for the specific medical advantages afforded by sterilization.
- Neutering does not affect learned behavior. If a dog has learned to hate letter carriers, neutering will not remove that hatred. It also will not make a guard dog passive or make a fearful dog less likely to bite you. Likewise, if Fido is a trained obedience hound or hunter, neutering will not make the animal stupid or cowardly.

- Neutering will not ruin a dog's tendency to protect his property or family. The suggestion that neutering will make the dog docile is not true. That is why sterilization is not an automatic cure for any type of aggression.
- Neutered cats are much less likely to fight other cats. Feline aggression is a serious cause of chronic battle damage that can lead to abscesses and infection.
- Roaming is a major cause of death for dogs and cats. Wandering pets are often hit by cars, abused by disgruntled neighbors or exposed to diseases and parasites. If your dog or cat regularly leaves your property to roam the neighborhood, it is unlikely to die of natural causes.

Puppy mills and children's pets: The beat goes on

Woody was born in a wire cage about three feet off the ground. His mother and father were both purebred Cocker Spaniels. The man who owned them had many dogs like Woody's parents. The man had been "farming" puppies for about ten years—it sure beat trying to raise corn.

Woody's mother, Sadie, had been at the farm for six years. Woody and his two sisters were her eighth litter, or "crops" as the man liked to call them. Her first family bought her from a pet shop, but had to take her to the pound when they moved out of state. The man "adopted" her for $25 and signed a contract to have her spayed. The man tossed the contract away and laughed at the thought of spaying a prime breeding animal. It was an easy task to fake her A.K.C. registration so her puppies would "have papers."

For the first few weeks, Woody's existence was confined to huddling close to his mother and litter mates. The only protection from the cold winter rains was a rusted sheet of tin that was wired haphazardly to the top of the cage. As his eyes and ears started to function, he noticed a large shape move past his cage. It was the man tending his crops.

Woody had his first contact with the man at about four weeks of age. He had never before actually been touched by a human. Woody shrank back in terror as a giant paw engulfed him and pulled him from the cage. He tried to bite the hand that held him, but the man shook him roughly and then tossed him back in the cage. The days that followed included more handling by humans. The man knew that taming the pups made them more marketable. His first litters had been so fearful that he could not sell them. He hired a neighbor girl to come and play with the puppies. His pups soon gained a reputation for being gentle. The pet stores liked that.

When Woody reached six weeks of age the man put him in a large plastic crate in the back of his truck. He selected several pups from other cages and added them to the harvest. The man drove his load quickly to a buyer in Kansas City. To get the pups to market for the Christmas rush, it was necessary to ship them by the middle of November.

The next day was a blur of wild sights and sounds. Woody was shipped, along with 20 other pups, by plane to Phoenix. From the relative quiet of the farm he was thrust overnight into a glass and steel cage in a shopping mall.

Woody stayed in his cage for exactly three weeks. A sign in the window announced, "A.K.C. Cocker Spaniel—$450.00." On Christmas Eve a man and woman came to the shop and asked to see Woody. They were told that he had papers and all of his shots. Woody's adorable appearance was the most powerful sales pitch of all—he went home with the couple.

The next morning the family gathered around the Christmas tree. The kids, Tommy and Lisa, had finished opening their presents when their father announced that he had another surprise for the family. He went into the garage and brought back Woody, complete with a Santa hat on his head. For 30 minutes Woody was mauled by the kids. They were overjoyed at having a puppy of their own. Lisa accidentally dropped him twice, while Tommy tried to ram Woody with his new radio-controlled monster truck.

His first few weeks with the family went poorly. Because of his early experience living in a cage, Woody could not grasp the idea of eliminating outdoors. Woody could not be house-trained. The family suffered through his improper elimination until finally the mother put her foot down—Woody became an outdoor dog.

Soon, he was further prevented from coming inside because he was always filthy. When the kids tried to play with him he would frantically try to jump on them in greeting. He knocked

Tommy down and accidentally scratched the child's face. This time the father put his foot down—Woody went to the pound.

The pound had a familiar feeling for Woody—it reminded him of his puppyhood. The wire cages were roomier than he remembered, but the smells were similar. Woody was adopted and returned three times. No one wanted a house dog that eliminated in the house. After the third try, the shelter got the message—Woody was not adoptable. Woody was put to sleep the next day.

That morning, half a continent away, the man went out to feed his dogs. He dumped some kibble in the food tray in Sadie's cage. Yes, sir, he thought, that Sadie had already pumped out over 20 pups. Not a bad return on a $25 investment. She would deliver again soon and the pups would be ready for sale by Christmas. The man smiled at the thought.

When guard dogs go wrong

Dan was burglarized twice in one week. In order to sleep soundly at night he did what any red-blooded American would—he got a watch dog. Bruno was a large shaggy Shepherd mix that Dan saw advertised in the classifieds. The original owner said that Bruno was too aggressive to trust around strangers. Dan bought the dog at once.

Dan took Bruno home and put the dog in the backyard. He bought some dog food, a big leather collar with spikes on it and a dog-house. He tacked "Beware of Dog" and "Attack Dog on Duty" signs on his fence. With Bruno in his back yard, Dan slept soundly for the first time in months. His bliss lasted almost a week—that's when Bruno bit the neighbor's son, Jimmy.

Jimmy had been playing Frisbee with his older brother. When the Frisbee sailed over the fence, Jimmy hopped after it. He didn't know about Bruno. His first indication that anything was wrong was when he tried to hop back over the fence. His leg suddenly seemed heavy. He must have caught his pants leg on something. As Jimmy looked down he realized that it was the other way around—something had caught his pants. A big shaggy snarling animal was whipsawing his leg back and forth. Jimmy tried to kick the dog away with his other leg but Bruno simply leaped higher and grabbed the back of the boy's thigh. Jimmy's brother grabbed a pool pole and succeeded in getting Bruno to let go of Jimmy's leg so that Jimmy could get over the fence.

Dan heard the commotion and grinned. He imagined the look of surprise on the burglar's face when Bruno came after him. Dan hustled to the back window to watch the action. By the time he got there, Bruno was trotting back to the house. Dan wrongly assumed that the dog had done a good deed and praised him lavishly.

The next morning, Dan got a call from an attorney. The attorney started asking him some very odd questions, such as: Did Dan have homeowner's insurance? No? What was the name of his attorney? Dan interrupted and asked what business it was whether or not he had insurance. As the lawyer recounted the full version of the past evening's events a glimmer of realization hit Dan. Bruno had attacked the neighbor kid rather than a prowler. The last thing he heard the lawyer say was something about "strict liability."

Dan's experience is more common than most would believe. According to the Humane Society of the United States, more than a million dog bites are reported annually. It is estimated that as many as five times that many bites go unreported.

Although most people have played some role in a dog attack, few people understand the full extent of the owner's responsibility. In most states, owners are held strictly liable for the actions of their pets. This means that under almost any circumstances the owner is responsible for any actual damages. The cost of emergency room treatment and plastic surgery can be many thousands of dollars. If the owner had reason to know that the animal had a tendency to bite people, the victim may also receive punitive damages totaling many thousands of dollars more. Signs that warn of an "Attack Dog on Duty," rather than relieving the owner of liability, may actually convince a jury that the owner knew the animal was dangerous.

Insurance companies usually take the brunt of this process. A mildly disfiguring scar on a child's face can easily cost over $100,000. Even if the dog was provoked, the insurance company may decide to settle out of court rather than take the case to trial. If the victim is a disfigured child, it may sway a jury into awarding huge damages, regardless of who is actually at fault.

Acquiring a dog as a defender or guardian is common. Realizing the full extent of the responsibilities of ownership is quite uncommon. It is ironic that so many people get a dog to protect their possessions without realizing that the animal's actions could actually put them out on the street.

The fly, the windshield and the dog: Need I say more?

"Stop that! You could put somebody's eye out." From rubber band gunfights to epic battles with makeshift "swords" our childhood fun was often halted by parental warnings of accidental blindness. Strangely, this paranoia would cease once the family entered a speeding automobile. Rusty, the family Cocker Spaniel, would serenely thrust his head out the window, ears flapping in the breeze. No one ever mentioned that his behavior could "put an eye out."

Before you assume that this is an exaggeration, look up "Auto Glass" in the Yellow Pages. All of those window fixers make their livings replacing windshields broken by flying rocks and debris. While almost every driver knows the relief of watching a rock fly straight at them and then bounce harmlessly off the windshield, some seem to think that dogs are immune to rock damage.

Rocks are not the only flying debris that can ruin Rusty's day. Even a small bug can do serious damage to an animal's eye or the back of the throat. A larger insect, such as a bumblebee, can cause severe injury or blindness. Gravel, dust and smog can cause a spectrum of problems, from minor irritation to serious damage.

Another obvious danger for unprotected road pets is being ejected from the vehicle during an accident. In Phoenix, a truck crossing a freeway overpass collided with another car. An adult Rottweiler, unsecured in the back of the truck, was launched onto the freeway below. The dog struck a passing car, causing it to crash. The driver of the car was seriously injured, and almost lost an arm.

Though the open bed of a pickup truck is the most obvious source of ejected pets, the open window of an automobile can be just as dangerous. In Seattle, a Bouvier De Flandres (a large shaggy dog) suddenly lunged past his owner and leaped from the car—at 65 miles per hour. As the dog rolled and skidded to a halt, several cars almost collided in order to avoid the beast. Fortunately the dog's thick coat protected it from injury.

Voluntary escape from a vehicle is more common than most people believe. At traffic lights, dogs may leap from their truck to chase or attack another animal. They may also simply exit the vehicle and run off. These mundane examples are not the only possibilities that exist when dogs become "road warriors." Several years ago, the canine mascot of a major beer company was attacked during a parade by two Pit Bull Terriers. The dogs had jumped from the back of their owner's pickup truck and leaped onto the vintage beer wagon where the mascot was riding. Though the beer wagon dog was not seriously injured, one wonders what could have happened if the marauders had attacked the team of huge draft horses that were pulling the wagon, instead of the dog.

In response to this problem, some states have enacted laws requiring that animals be secured if they are transported in an open truck. While pet lovers are sincere in passing such legislation, laws of this type do little to stop the problem. Police agencies rarely have enough money to allow them to focus on unsecured pets. It is even more difficult to take such a law seriously in states where it is still legal for children to ride in the bed of a pickup.

For those owners who would like to provide a safe means of travel for their animal, there are several alternatives. Using an airline carrier or heavy wire cage to contain the pet is a good idea—if it is secured. During an accident, unsecured carriers and cages simply become larger and stronger projectiles that fly from your truck.

Another option is to use a specially designed tie-down for the dog. Several companies make straps that allow you to secure the dog behind the cab of the pickup. While these straps do allow the dog more security, they may still allow the dog to fall over the side of the bed. Correct installation is necessary to prevent Fido from accidentally hanging himself.

For car owners, several pet supply catalogs feature safety screens that allow your dog to feel the wind in his face without risking injury or escape. Special safety seats and harnesses are now available that can secure your pet in the event of an accident or sudden stop.

As society changes from primarily rural living to urban, we are sometimes slow in changing our ways. The sight of a sheep dog riding on top of a slow moving farm truck has little to do with a Rottweiler precariously balanced in the bed of a "tricked out" mini-truck on the freeway. Failing to secure your pet while traveling in an automobile may not be against the law—its just a bad idea.

Purebred-schmurebred:
Get a dog that is "bred good"
not one with "good breeding"

If someone tells you that his dog has "papers," nod your head and smile. When he tells you that his dog is a rare, silver tipped Carthaginian Mastiff and that he is one of only three in the United States, nod your head. Then say something like "Oh, how fortunate for you." If he claims that his dog is directly descended from Fluffy, personal war dog of Hannibal the Great, you should continue to listen politely. If he tells you that this rare and valuable dog was given to him for a fraction of its real value, you don't have to be polite anymore. You may feel free to belly laugh—as long as you are wearing protective gear.

One of the great myths about purebred animals is that they have intrinsic cash value. In a country where 90% of the dogs and cats born each year do not survive to see their first birthday, there is a glut on the market. The truth is that rather than being valuable commodities, the vast majority are monetarily worthless.

These realities of supply and demand are usually unknown or ignored. For example, several million people surrender purebred pets to animal shelters each year. When the shelter worker cautions them that there is no guarantee that the animal will be adopted, the owner often says, "Oh, I'm sure he'll get adopted. He has papers." When asked to leave a donation, this type of pet owner is likely to be offended and say, "What? But I'm giving you a very valuable animal! Can't you see that he's a purebred?" The irony of giving an animal away while insisting that it is valuable is rarely perceived by the owner.

One of the reasons for the belief that all purebreds are valuable is that a very small percentage of purebred animals are actually worth fantastic sums of money. If a dog wins the Westminster Kennel Club dog show in New York, subsequent stud fees or puppy sales can be worth many thousands of dollars. The sight of tuxedos, formal gowns and celebrities at a nationally televised dog show causes many people to assume that it represents the norm, rather than the exception.

Another source of misinformation is the recent trend of using top dog show winners in television commercials endorsing pet food. The advertisements foster the notion that breeders of champion dogs live in rustic country estates and just watch all the money roll in from the sale of their animals. For the general public, the image brings the mistaken conclusion that breeding creates dogs and dogs create wealth. No one dreams that the rustic estate was probably rented for the commercial and that the breeder will probably make more from the commercial than from selling dogs. Few people realize that competing in the "dog game" is very expensive. A top competitor could easily need a six-figure budget in order to compete enough to stay on top. Only a small fraction of dog-show people ultimately make big money from their dogs. Most breeders barely cover expenses or may actually take a loss.

In this highly competitive sport, breeders may become more interested in winning than breeding good dogs. In order to improve a bloodline, a breeder might pay a small fortune for a particular dog. It is often assumed that breeders are focused on animals that will be healthier or smarter. In some cases, they may buy a dog purely because it is apricot colored, has a broader head or a thicker coat.

When an offspring of this "breed-to-win" type of champion is sold, the new owner assumes that the pup is the by-product of greatness and is therefore valuable. The truth may be that the pup's only championship attribute is apricot colored hair. The chance that any other breeder would want to use an unproved pet animal for breeding is small. Unless the new owner is willing to compete with the animal at dog shows and is able to win, the high purchase price is a waste of money.

Assuming that an animal is valuable because it has pedigree papers, a fancy name and looks like a "show dog," is a naive belief. Most animals are financial liabilities rather than assets. Their true value most often lies in the miraculous companionship and bond that is possible between different species—and they are far better than your checkbook at keeping your feet warm.

Were you born "good with animals?" Or did you learn it?

There are quite a few people out there who consider themselves "naturally good with animals." It is a rare shock to one of these people when they meet an animal who happens to be "naturally bad with people who are naturally good with animals." The inevitable result is a nasty bite wound and a shattered ego. The belief that being good with animals is an innate quality can give false confidence to some, while excluding others from the enjoyment of animal companionship.

The term "naturally good with animals" should really refer to a level of expertise rather than a genetic endowment. Usually the person in question just happens to have been raised on a farm, competed in rodeos, 4-H, dog shows, or is the child of an animal lover. The fact that the person handles animals well is invariably the result of a simple formula—the person has handled lots of animals. Conversely, people who are not good with animals are primarily those with the least experience.

For people who are not good with animals, encounters with non-humans can range from mild annoyance to true terror. For some, a petting zoo or pony ride is as frightening as a real-life Jurassic Park. A popular, but mistaken belief that displaying fear can cause an animal to attack complicates this reaction. For someone who is terrified of animals, hiding the fear is impossible. The only solution is to avoid their fear by avoiding animals, entirely.

Ironically, it is often the person who tries to ignore animals that seems to attract them most. The reason for this reaction is simple. Many animals perceive direct eye contact as a threat or challenge. People who try to ignore animals intentionally avoid eye contact. This passive display acts as a lure to most animals. Despite human complaints about simply wanting to be left alone, the animal views passive behavior as an open invitation for greeting and affection.

The first step toward becoming good with animals is to realize that good handling is a simple matter of expanding your knowledge. The first thing to know is that different species may react differently to the same situation. For instance, a dog is usually pleased to have its belly rubbed. Doing the same thing to a cat may cause the animal to grab you with its claws and either bite or scratch you.

Another important consideration when handling pets depends on the age of the animal. Both dogs and cats move their young by picking them up by the scruff of the neck. Though both species tolerate this behavior as infants, only cats will allow you to do this to them as adults. Many dogs react to someone grabbing their scruff by inflicting a bite to the offending wrist.

While there are many differences among species, some reactions are almost universal. Most species react to eye contact as a threat or challenge. This common reaction is responsible for the belief that animals will attack if they sense fear. In reality, the animal attacks because it perceives the fearful human stare as a threat. If the frightened human avoids staring "wide-eyed" at the beast, his chances of getting bitten are greatly reduced. By using peripheral vision, the person can still watch the animal without triggering a bite.

One of the most important general rules for handling animals is to give them plenty of warning before you touch them. This rule is especially important if you know nothing of the animal's temperament. In public, it is both dangerous and rude to assume that you may interact with someone's pet. If you don't wait to find out if "the little dog bites," you may find out the hard way.

For those of you who are intimidated by strange animals, there are plenty of opportunities to learn better handling skills. Many animal shelters, veterinary hospitals and kennels accept volunteer help or would be willing to give you instruction. Almost every city has clubs for lovers of purebred dogs and cats that can help you learn safe and humane handling skills. Attending dog, cat and livestock shows can put you in touch with people who are both skilled and humane in their treatment of animals. The more you work at it the faster you may become "unnaturally good with animals."

Life at all costs: A lesson learned

Inky, the Lab, lurched up from the ground. His rear legs were wobbly and unsteady. His muzzle was a uniform white that faded to gray around his face and eyes. His coat was a lackluster black. He looked as if he were one step away from a heart attack. Inky was seventeen.

Inky's owner, Sally, had been kidding herself for a long time about Inky's condition. Her parents had given Inky to her on her eighth birthday. He had been a little black lump of fur in her Christmas stocking. Now, at 25, she could barely imagine life without Inky. They had grown up together.

Inky's hips weren't the only things that were starting to fail. His eyes were the telltale milky blue of cataracts. His kidneys and bladder were barely able to process or retain his urine. He could no longer sleep at the foot of her bed.

As Inky slowly wasted away, Sally's boyfriend became concerned. He asked if she thought it was time to put Inky to sleep. She called him insensitive and demanded to know if he'd like to be put down just because he had a little gray hair. She asked if he would put her down one day just because she was old.

Soon after the argument, Inky lost all control of his bladder. Sally had been in the habit of allowing him in at night to sleep on a heated pad on the back porch. She was horrified one day to find the electrically heated pad soaked in urine and a burn mark on Inky's hip. She put a heat lamp in Inky's doghouse and stopped bringing him in the house.

Inky's skin was starting to cause him some trouble as well. He began to develop scabs and runny sores on his paws and back. The skin on his rump became thick and looked like several doughnuts circling his tail. It was becoming hard to find a place to touch him that was not affected.

Sally did not take Inky to the vet. She was afraid her veterinarian would tell her to put Inky down. She didn't want to hear that.

The skin problem continued to grow over Inky's body. Sally tried home remedies and shampoos that came from the pet shop. Inky's system had no way to fight back. The chemicals in the medications were doing more damage to him than the mites that were infesting his body.

On his eighteenth birthday, Inky had a small stroke. Sally came home from work and found him struggling to get up. Each time he attempted to stand, he fell against the side of his dog house. She rushed to him and tried to hold him down. His distorted sense of balance rebelled at her efforts and he struggled harder to get up.

Sally could not escape the truth any longer. Inky must see a veterinarian. She bundled him into her car and took him to a clinic several miles away. Sally intentionally called a veterinarian that she didn't know. She was finally seeing Inky's condition for what it was. She was ashamed to let her veterinarian see him.

Sally barely noticed the stares of the people at the clinic. For the first time in years, she cradled Inky in her arms without a concern for staining her clothes. The technicians and office workers were repulsed by Inky's appearance. How could anyone be so cruel—to let him live in that condition. This must have taken years of neglect, they thought.

Sally cried slowly as the doctor prepared to put Inky to sleep. The veterinarian chose not to confront this woman with her actions. As Inky lapsed into unconsciousness, Sally turned and left the room. She paid the bill at the counter, and hurried to her car. She sat in the driver's seat and sobbed.

Sally had never intended to hurt Inky. She simply could not face the thought of losing him. Though it was too late for Inky, Sally finally learned the hardest lesson of all—it is the quality of life that makes it worth living.

Amazing feats of animal learning

During the Gulf War in Iraq, news programs flooded viewers with video tape of hi-tech "smart bombs" that unerringly hit their targets. It might surprise you to know that during World War II, a group of scientists invented the first "smart bomb," that could guide itself to the target. Over 50 years ago, behavioral scientists developed a bomb that had the "inhuman" accuracy of over 90%. This skill level was 30% better than the best bombardiers had achieved. The generals who were shown the "smart bomb" were fascinated by it, until they learned its secret. Inside the bomb were three pigeons trained to peck keys that could change the bomb's course. The generals were afraid to develop the bomb because they believed that the public might assume that the pigeons were not the only "bird brains" connected with such a venture.

Although this "smart bomb" project was judged to be a wacky idea, the truth is that it probably would have worked. When humans combine good training techniques with animal "know-how," many amazing things can be accomplished. A variation of the pigeon bomb is used in rescue attempts at sea. The method utilizes a bird to spot the yellow life vests of pilots who have been lost at sea. The bird sits perched in a small observation window on a naval airplane. When the bird spots something yellow, it pecks a key to alert the crew. Pigeons can see yellow at distances far beyond the range of the human eye.

Pigeons are not the only animals that have been taught to do unusual things. Recent developments in arson investigation include dogs that sniff out the burned remains of flammable substances. The dogs allow investigators to quickly pinpoint the focus of an investigation and save hundreds of man hours. Other novel uses for canine noses include termite-sniffing dogs and U.S. Customs Service dogs that can detect contraband fruit, vegetables and plants.

Another unusual animal task is the practice of using dolphins and seals to find objects underwater. Free-swimming marine mammals can identify objects at depths of over 800 feet. Recent advances in this behavioral technology allow dolphins to be fitted with miniature video cameras that allow humans on the surface to see exactly what the animal sees. In a single day, seals and dolphins can cover an area that would require weeks of searching if done by human divers.

This cooperative nature of the human/animal bond is not exclusively established by the human partner. Small groups of dolphins along the Atlantic coast of Brazil herd fish into the waiting nets of fishermen. The fishermen do not deliberately reinforce the dolphin's behavior, yet this phenomenon has been observed for over 100 years. It is possible that the dolphins instigated this relationship. Several generations of dolphins and fishermen have each passed the behavior along to their young.

Developing new roles for animals in human society is not without controversy. In Australia, pigeons were taught to peck a key to reject defective parts on a production line. This project was developed as a way to relieve human workers from the tedium of the job. The project was stopped by protesters who said that reinforcing birds to do such a tedious task was inhumane. The result was that humans were rehired to take over the "inhumane" work.

A group of trainers working for the government developed a crow that could follow a red laser dot and carry a miniature camera to photograph whatever was there. The animal was then recalled with a blue recall beacon, so that the bird and film could be recovered. In a similar project, a bird was taught to wear a harness that held a tiny microphone and transmitter. The red laser spot would be aimed at a window ledge near someone who was being watched. The bird would fly to the spot and then pull a retaining pin that dropped the transmitter on the ledge. The suspect could be "bugged" in almost any location and few people would suspect a crow of being a spy.

As modern training techniques create more ingenious animal skills, our social contact with animals will increase. It is no longer remarkable to see animal-assisted therapy in hospitals or service dogs helping their masters in public. This development can both enhance our lives as well as give new meaning to everyday occurrences. For instance, the next time someone says " a little bird told me," it just could be the truth.

Owners of problem pets:
Honesty is the best policy

Pugsly, the Yorkshire Terrier, is almost three years old. He is small, cute, cuddly and already neutered. He knows how to sit, lie down, come and walk on a leash. He does not chew on shoes, jump on guests or dart out the front door. He loves children and cats. His original owners paid several hundred dollars for him when he was a puppy, but that was three families ago. His current owners have advertised in the paper and are willing to give him to anyone who wants him, absolutely free. They have decided that if no one takes him by Friday, Pugsly goes to the county pound.

If this description has you reaching for the telephone to offer to save little Pugsly, be forewarned—Pugsly's only fault is that he marks his territory by urinating on the furniture. He is already neutered, so the behavior is not the result of testosterone coursing through his little body. Neither is it a simple house training problem. Be aware that if you take him, he will lift his leg on your furniture too. Soon your house will smell exactly like a kennel or the homes of the other four families who tried to live with him. Do you think he will be adopted again?

If Pugsly's fate troubles you, how about Reggie? He's a purebred Dalmatian with blue eyes. His breeder considered him the pick of the litter until it was discovered that Reggie was totally deaf. When the breeder mentioned to his friend, Sally, that Reggie would be put to sleep, Sally stepped in and took Reggie home. Now, eight months later, Reggie is a ten month old, deaf Dalmatian who cannot come when called, is still not house trained, and has destroyed most of Sally's backyard. Did I mention that last week Reggie nipped the neighbors' little boy? Sally is about to deliver her first child and isn't willing to take the chance that Reggie might harm her baby. Reggie, too, is going to the shelter—unless you would like to take him.

One of the sad side effects of pet ownership is the disposal of maladapted pets. Many people adopt an animal for all the right reasons, only to find out that the animal cannot adapt to life in human society. Once they come to grips with their inability to live with the pet, some difficult decisions must be made.

Should Pugsly's most recent family be honest about why they are giving him up? If they tell the truth, they are faced with the assurance that he will be put to sleep. If they lie, he will stain and mark someone else's house until they get rid of him—or worse. Either way, Pugsly will ultimately be destroyed, abandoned or abused.

Reggie's owner, Sally, has a similar problem—with a twist. If she admits that Reggie is deaf, he will probably be put to sleep. What if someone at the shelter feels sorry for him, as she did, and takes him home? Reggie has some other problems now in addition to his deafness. What if he bit another child? Could Sally be sued because she failed to tell the shelter that Reggie had previously bitten someone? The real issue is whether or not Sally can make the decision to be honest about Reggie's condition and his behavior.

All too often, pet owners avoid the tough decision of having their pet destroyed by covering up the animal's problem. Many dogs and cats are turned in at animal shelters under the fiction that the family is moving. While this is a convenient excuse, it does not hide the truth very well. If they are truthfully moving, they will haul old car parts, washing machines and antique anvils to their new home. Regardless of size, weight or inconvenience, the family would never consider leaving anything of value behind. That's where their true feelings show through—they do not value their animal. Another common excuse is that some family member is allergic to the animal or that it can't get along with other pets. These owners kid themselves into believing that there is some special person out there who won't mind the smell of dog urine in their living room or a childless farmer who has dreamed of owning a deaf dog.

Owning a pet is an experience that can enhance one's life. Accepting responsibility for another creature is the price of that enhancement. The best advice for those who are faced with choosing to put a pet to sleep is to get a second opinion. Consult with a veterinarian to make sure that the problem is beyond your control. If the animal is potentially dangerous, consult an attorney regarding potential liability if you sell or give the animal away. If you are forced to give the animal up, the old cliché remains true, honesty is the best policy.

Make sure you get your money's worth from training

Bill and Mary bought an expensive Labrador Retriever that they named Jeepers. Bill wanted a dog that he could enjoy as a pet, as well as a hunter. He paid $500 to a trainer to take the dog for a month of intensive training. While at the trainer's kennel, Jeepers was supposed to learn basic obedience as well as how to retrieve birds.

When Bill got the dog back, he was surprised by what his money had bought him. Jeepers stoutly refused to obey even the simplest commands. On Jeeper's second day home, Mary scolded the dog and told him to get out of the garbage. Jeepers tried to bite her. Bill knew something was very wrong.

The next day, Bill called a group that handles complaints about local businesses. They had no reports of complaints about the trainer. They advised Bill to file suit in small claims court. Bill was justifiably upset. He decided to skip the court battle.

According to recent studies, 75% of animals released to animal shelters are taken there because of unacceptable behavior. As Bill found out, though, the decision to provide behavioral care for a pet is not enough. To give your animal adequate training you must be an informed consumer. Here are several things you must consider before hiring a training service.

Your first decision is between private or group instruction. Groups have the advantage of low cost, but lack individual attention. If you or your dog needs special handling, you may not get it. Depending on location, the average cost is $50 for eight weekly sessions and may run as high as $100 or more. Group instruction may vary from just a few students to more than 20.

Private instruction allows you to learn at a rate geared to you and your dog. Many of the most common behavioral complaints are not covered by groups, but are the focus of private instruction. The average fee is about $350, but can range from $200 to $2000 or more.

While the total price of private training appears much higher than group classes, the actual rate may be closer than you think. A class of ten pupils will each get about 1/10th of the instructor's time, or about 48 minutes of private instruction over a typical eight week course. While the $50 fee looked cheap compared to the private training, it really was not. Your 48 minutes of individual attention cost you $57 per hour—about the same rate as the private instructor. The other seven class hours may be spent watching someone else get help, or falling behind because your dog is distracted or nervous. On top of that, the group instructor got a total of $500 for eight hours work—a rate of $62.00 per hour.

The real issue of cost and effectiveness rests with the overall results of the service. Many pet owners benefit from traditional classes in the park. Stubborn or difficult to train animals may not learn under group conditions. As with most things, a little research may save you time and money later.

- If the trainer advertises behavior modification and problem-solving, ask for veterinary references. Many medical conditions mimic behavioral problems. If the trainer does not have a good working relationship with at least one veterinarian, he may not know the difference. You and your dog will pay the price for his lack of knowledge.
- The best dog trainer may not be the best "people trainer." If the trainer does not leave you with practical skills after the program is completed, the service is of little use. Shortly after the trainer goes away your dog's skill will leave too.
- To take advantage of any training course, be prepared to participate and practice. Much of the success of any program depends on you. If you want to play the fiddle, or train your dog, you have to practice.
- Be wary of harsh training measures directed at the dogs or at the students. Browbeating and humiliation are not good tools

to teach humans or animals. If you feel uncomfortable about the way your dog is being handled, say something immediately. If the trainer cannot give you a reasonable assurance that the technique is safe and effective— don't do it.

Mobile "baggage" requires good I.D.

One of the worst feelings in the world is the sense of dread that comes when a pet runs away from home. When the kids forget to close the gate, or a workman leaves a door open, your pampered pet is suddenly on its own in a very dangerous world.

Getting Fluffy or Fido back is often dependent upon your level of preparation beforehand. If you have a secure collar and current tags on your animal, you have increased your chance of getting the critter back. For unidentified animals, the way home is almost impossible to trace.

The primary safety factor for a lost pet is an appropriate collar. Cats are often left without collars because people are afraid that the collar could potentially choke the animal if it caught on a branch or chain link fence. While this is certainly a possibility, the realities of automobiles, aggressive dogs, starvation and disease are far more likely fates. Dog owners face the same difficulty if their dog routinely wears a choke chain. If you fear the possibility that your pet will become snagged by its collar, use a "break away" collar for your cat, and a nylon web collar for your dog.

The next important tool for protecting your pet is current identification. The most common mistake regarding identification is to fail to provide any, or to forget to have current information on the tags. Of stray animals that are ultimately destroyed at shelters, 90% are not wearing tags. Animals wearing identification have a 90% chance of being returned to their owner. Having outdated information such as a disconnected phone number on your pet's tag is not going to help the animal get back home again.

Ironically, house pets are most commonly left unidentified. "Since Fluffy never goes outside," goes the reasoning, "why should she have a tag?" It is precisely this pampered, exclusively indoor cat or dog that needs to get home, pronto. Having lived within the same four walls all their lives, these pets are most at risk on the street. It only takes one careless workman or delivery person to accidentally let a pampered pet escape.

The type of identification you select is also an important ingredient in getting your pet back. All across the country, dogs are required to display a current rabies tag. This tag has a number on it, but not your vital statistics. If a person finds your dog after regular business hours, the number is useless. To be even safer, put a personalized tag on the animal in addition to the rabies tag. This way a person who finds your pet can call you directly. This saves animal control the trouble of impounding your pet—and charging you an impound fee.

Sometimes poorly designed or attached tags offer a false feeling of security. Tags that dangle from a split ring or "S" hook may get caught on an obstructions like a fence or a bush. As Fido struggles to get free, the tag will pull loose. One alternative is to have the tag riveted to the collar. This can be done at most shoe shops, or with an inexpensive riveting tool.

Another option is to have your pet tattooed. There may be five Labrador Retrievers at the pound at any time, but only one with your driver's license number tattooed on his inner thigh. Since this practice is still fairly uncommon, tattoos are seldom looked for by animal control personnel. While it may be of limited use in getting your animal home, it is certainly positive proof that you own the dog.

If your pet does escape, contact your nearest animal control shelter immediately. Find out the names of private animal welfare agencies in the area that also hold stray pets. Your best chance of reclaiming your pet is to visit every local shelter, daily. It is not safe to assume that shelter personnel can correctly identify your pet over the phone. I know of one case in which a stray Irish Wolfhound was impounded as a Great Dane mixed with Airedale Terrier. The owner was mistakenly told that no Irish Wolfhounds were in the kennels. That dog almost lost his life over a simple mistake. The only sure way to find out if your pet is at the shelter, is to go there and see for yourself.

Another way to plan ahead is to prepare a set of high quality black and white photos of your pet—before the animal gets lost. Make sure that they reproduce well when photocopied. If Fido or Fluffy gets lost, you can make posters to hang up in the neighborhood. Posters work best when they are in places most likely to be read. Laundromats, public bulletin boards and shopping areas are good. Posters on telephone poles are often unreadable at 50 miles per hour.

Newspaper classified advertisements can reach a wider audience than just your neighborhood. If you own a rare breed, stick to a simple description of the beast. Few people will know what your registered Gucci hound looks like. Offering a reward may also help to draw attention to your pet's predicament.

Finding a pet after it is lost on the streets can be a time consuming and difficult process. The best way to protect your animals is to make sure they never escape in the first place—and make sure Fido and Fluffy are wearing good identification in case they do.

Part 5:
Acquiring a Pet

How to pick a pet

Buying a pet should be the result of a rational decision. Despite the importance and difficulty of selecting the perfect pet, it is often an impulse purchase. The average person decides to get an animal using the same criteria that one uses when selecting a corndog at the state fair. Is it warm? Can I have it now? How much does it cost? For those of you with a more cautious nature, here are some tips to help you make your decision.

Purchasing an animal is a buyer's market. The huge excess of animals in this country allows you to get a wonderful pet for a very reasonable amount of money. If you simply want any pet you can get you hands on, there are many available, absolutely free.

Your first decision should be what type of animal you really want. This may seem absurdly basic, but the more thought you give to your specific desires, the better able you will be to find the perfect pet. Many people are attracted to animals for impractical or sentimental reasons. The fact that your ex-beau had a lovely blue Chow is a lousy reason for you to buy one. The idealized memory of that other animal may bear no resemblance to the little creature that you wind up with. You will eventually be disappointed with the animal because it does not live up to your unrealistic expectations.

If you work 16 hours per day, seven days per week, you may want to avoid high maintenance animals such as dogs. You will have a better chance with an animal that does not require as much attention. Cats, rodents, fish and reptiles are better suited to live this lifestyle.

After you select the type of pet you want, you will need to find a source for the animal. You should try to see as many examples of your ideal pet as possible. The most common sources of animals are private individuals, animal shelters, pet shops and breeders. Each source comes with advantages and disadvantages.

Individuals: The main disadvantage of buying an animal from a stranger is that you may be buying someone else's problem. The person may also be highly motivated to say anything to get you to take the animal off their hands. The main advantages are relatively low purchase price, and the knowledge that most problems are correctable. If you purchase the animal with the stipulation that it must pass a health examination by your veterinarian, this can be a good source for a pet.

Animal shelters: The main advantages of adopting from a shelter are broad selection and the knowledge that you have helped in reducing the surplus pet population. You may also be able to buy an animal for a fraction of its original price. Be aware that animals at shelters are of no particular quality. If a puppy mill animal is defective when sold at a pet shop, it does not suddenly become wonderful when it is taken to an animal shelter. There is a subtle hypocrisy in the policy of most animal shelters. They attack pet shops for selling "defective" animals, but want you to buy the same animal from them once the original owner gives it up.

Pet Shops: It has become popular and "humane" to attack pet shops as a source of animals. While there is no doubt that abuses exist in the pet industry, there are some pet shops who provide animals that are as healthy and long-lived as any purebred with champion bloodlines. You would be better off researching individual pet shops rather than assuming that all of them are bad. Price is the most obvious disadvantage to pet shops. While a breeder might sell a pet-quality puppy for $100, the pet shop must sell for three times that to make a profit.

Another disadvantage is the fact that most pet shops will not reveal the source of their animals. It is ironic that a pet shop will charge you an extravagant amount of money because an animal is purebred, i.e. of known parentage, but will not tell you what that parentage is until after you buy the pet. This is similar to charging a fortune for an old pair of sneakers because they were once owned by a famous movie star—then refusing to tell you who the star was until after you pay for the shoes.

Private Breeders: Theoretically, a dedicated breeder is most likely to have sound, healthy animals. The truth is that there are no requirements or objective standards that will allow you to tell a good breeder from a bad one. So, while a private breeder has the best chance of breeding superior animals, they may not. Do not be impressed with blue ribbons that were gained because the animal looks good. If the breeder is primarily interested in looks, you may get a beautiful animal with lousy health. Try to find an experienced breeder who repeatedly emphasizes health and good temperament as the goals of his or her breeding program. Ask for references, both among satisfied customers and the breeder's veterinarian.

Selecting the proper pet is far more difficult than most people realize. Snap decisions and impulse buying should be avoided. The more time you spend before you buy, the better chance you have of finding the animal that is right for you.

Breed type is what you expect:
Your pet is what you get

Many pet owners have a love affair with "breed type." Cats, dogs, horses and heifers are all separated into distinct subdivisions—each possesses particular traits. By picking a particular breed, you may think you can know what to expect. In theory, it is a great idea. In practice, you may be in for a surprise.

Dog lore is filled with assumptions about different breeds. With complete smugness a friend might tell you that Basenjis don't bark, Dobermans are aggressive and Golden Retrievers have no faults at all.

This overly simplistic view is very common, but often wrong. Your dog may not fit any known description. Authorities that claim specific traits for a breed imply a consistency that does not exist. They would have you believe that Bassett Hounds roll from an assembly line somewhere like toaster ovens and televisions. Stamped on each little forehead is the inscription, "Inspected by Number 4." The next time you see one of those little stamps, you will know that your dog will conform to the standards perfectly and if it doesn't you can take it right back to the factory.

To illustrate the limitations of "breedology" a human comparison may be in order. My wife's particular breeding is half Irish and half Norwegian. According to the common conception of breed type, she should love lutefisk, a smelly fish cooked in milk, and have a bad temper. She actually hates lutefisk, and stopped throwing things at me several years ago.

Within any species of animal there is great diversity. Even within a given breed there can be wide differences. Persian Cats are supposed to like lying in a person's lap. I had to teach my cat, Moozer, to appreciate the finer points of lap-sitting. He simply would not stay put for even a few seconds. Is Moozer missing a gene, or is lap-sitting a learned behavior? One wonders what survival benefit is connected with sitting in human laps. Did prehistoric cats have an instinct to jump in the laps of cavemen for protection and affection?

The best use of breed type is in selecting the general physical appearance and abilities of your pet. Lightly built dogs are better for playing Frisbee than heavy-boned giants. If your passion is Frisbee, don't buy a Rottweiler. If you want a cat that will shed all over your furniture, get a long-haired cat like mine.

Claims of courage, intelligence and tolerance of children sound alluring but may be the idealized view of a dedicated enthusiast. Any connection between the description in a book and the breeding of your pet may be purely coincidental. Before selecting a pet, see as many of them as possible. If you have only seen one example of a Tasmanian Goola-Goola, you are betting that your animal will be the same. If you wind up with a Retriever that doesn't retrieve, a Basenji who barks or a Doberman who is afraid of his shadow, don't be disappointed. Give your pet the respect he deserves—as an individual.

Genetic trait or genetic trade-off

Imagine for a moment that your loving Springer Spaniel suddenly gets a distant look in his eye. Without warning, he attacks you viciously and then backs off. Instead of continuing to threaten you, he has a dazed look on his face as if he is unaware of what he has done. If you think your pet is crazy, you are right. His behavior is probably the result of a genetic disorder.

Breeding purebred animals is an old tradition. For thousands of years, animals have been selected for particular traits. From the sharp nose of a Blood Hound to the flat nose of the Persian Cat, selective breeding has retained the best examples of these traits—and the worst.

To illustrate the difficulty of breeding healthy animals, pretend you are a German Shepherd breeder. As with many breeds of dogs, they sometimes suffer from hip dysplasia—an often crippling condition. To breed dogs that will not have this disorder, you must first find a bloodline that is free of the defect. After you find these dysplasia-free German Shepherds, you breed your litter, secure in the knowledge that you will have healthy pups.

Unfortunately, while your pups may not become dysplastic, they develop epilepsy. Next you try to avoid epilepsy and get a litter that develops diabetes—and dysplasia. According to "Medical and Genetic Aspects of Purebred Dogs," by veterinarian Ross Clark and Joan Stainer, there are at least 25 genetic defects common to German Shepherds. Trying to avoid one of these problems risks acquiring one or more of the others.

German Shepherds are not alone in this genetic "Russian roulette." Miniature Poodles have over 26 known hereditary diseases, while Labrador Retrievers have at least 25. Even the best breeders have difficulty isolating healthy breeding pairs.

Cats do not escape this hereditary dilemma either. Flat-faced cats like Himalayans and Persians have a full set of teeth scrunched into a tiny jaw. Their nasal passages and sinuses are often malformed. Some defects in cats seem inconsequential. "Polydactylism" describes cats born with many toes. Their feet look like baseball gloves. This disorder does not debilitate the cat. Manx Cats, from the British Isles, are born without a tail. This seems harmless but may be a serious problem. Some tailless cats are also born without the proper nerve network in the rectal and anal regions. The result is a cat that may not have any ability to control its bowels.

Two other serious hereditary problems for cats are deafness and epilepsy. White cats with two blue eyes have about a 50% chance of being deaf. Epileptic cats may show no symptoms of the disease until they are adults.

The attraction for particular breeds of domesticated animals is universal. Each culture has developed its own image of how a cat or dog should look or act. Along with the wonderful physical and behavioral traits that have been passed down, grave illnesses and maladies have come along too.

The expertise to breed healthy, genetically sound animals is a rare commodity. Good breeders are dedicated and educated people who take every possible precaution to prevent birth defects. Before breeding animals for fun and profit, consult your veterinarian and experienced breeders to find out what it takes to do it right.

Reinforcement can reveal "secret" knowledge

Jay, the Retriever, got tossed in the pound. Three days later he was adopted and his new family named him Skeeter. Jay didn't really care whether they called him Skeeter or Beeter or any other name, as long as the called him for dinner.

Skeeter's new family took him home and got him "settled in." They marveled at how easy it was for him to adjust. They knew that they had a very bright dog on their hands. What they didn't know was that Jay was a former obedience and field trial champion.

Skeeter had no way to tell his new family that he knew over 25 spoken commands and about a dozen hand signals. He had been lost by his original owner after a car accident, six months before. Bedraggled and filthy, he was found by a man who wondered why anyone would let such a nice dog run loose. The man moved out of state and took the dog to the animal shelter as a last resort.

If only the family had known the right commands and hand signals, they would have been even more impressed with their new dog. One day, Julie, the family's daughter, made a remarkable discovery. She had some oyster crackers and started teasing Skeeter with them. First she would touch a cracker to his nose and then pull it back. Skeeter got very excited and then did something they had not seen before. He very deliberately rolled over. Julie squealed with delight and ran to her mother. "Skeeter rolled over! I offered him a cracker and he rolled over! Come watch him do it again!"

Julie's mother came in and watched her daughter tease the dog and then pull the treat away. This time Skeeter surprised both of them. Julie's hand accidentally curved in a circle that Skeeter recognized from his former life. He instantly bolted away from them and grabbed the newspaper off the coffee table and raced back to them with his prize. Julie and her mother were amazed at this behavior. This process of teasing Skeeter seemed to bring out a wealth of "new" behaviors.

"Try it again," said the mother, "let's see what else he knows."

For the next half hour, Julie and her mother alternately gasped in astonishment and howled with laughter at Skeeter's accomplishments. By merely teasing him repeatedly with the oyster crackers, they found out that he knew how to back up, spin left or right, paw the ground like Trigger and give a pretty good "high five." He also kept circling around Julie and ending up sitting by her side in the perfect "heel" position. On two occasions, Julie accidentally gave signals that Skeeter recognized. One was a hand signal that meant "nod your head;" the other was when Julie said, "Hey mom, watch this!" Skeeter heard the word "watch" and started to growl and bark at an imaginary danger.

Whenever Skeeter seemed to hang up on one behavior, Julie would simply say "Uh-uh" and tease him again. In no time Skeeter learned that the old behavior wasn't working anymore and that he should throw another one at her. Julie took notes and wrote down what signal seemed to "cause" which behavior.

Many people adopt or buy animals that have unknown histories. Any prior training is assumed to be lost, or is only elicited by accident. Julie's method of saying "Tell me what you know" is actually a long established technique of marine mammal trainers. First perfected by behavioral biologist Karen Pryor, this method can also be used to teach an animal to "give me something entirely new," and can easily be adapted for family pets.

Captivity rarely allows an animal the opportunity to use its mental capacities to the fullest. Structured play and training that utilizes the animal's ability to think can lead to a more full and satisfying relationship. Whether your goal is to explore the potential of a new pet or expand the behaviors of a pet that you have raised, finding out exactly what the dog knows can be a "rewarding" challenge.

Want a pet?
Choose the best and the brightest

Harley was a purebred Golden Retriever. At two years of age, he was in the prime of his life. He could expect many more years of service to his master. Then one day his life changed—his owner died in a car accident. Harley's owner had left specific instructions for Harley's future. He was to go to the owner's brother, Tim. Tim had other ideas. Tim was going through a divorce. Harley went to the pound.

The people at the shelter marveled at Harley. He was already neutered, perfectly trained, beautiful and healthy. He loved kids and other dogs. They had no doubt that Harley would be adopted quickly.

His first day at the shelter, a nice woman walked by who also marveled at Harley. She read the card that told of his attributes and thought that surely he would be adopted quickly.

She had decided to adopt from the shelter because of a national ad that showed a starving Shepherd puppy in a cage. The caption said that he was on "death row." The ad convinced her to go to the shelter and "save a life."

In the cage next to Harley was a very fearful, Shepherd-type puppy. It huddled at the back of the cage and shivered. It looked just like the pathetic "death row" puppy in the ad. The woman adopted the puppy instead of Harley. She knew that a dog like Harley would be adopted, but who would take a pitiful looking puppy? She was there to save a life. She lived through six years of locking her fearful dog outside whenever visitors came to the house. Finally the dog bit a child and was put to sleep.

Harley's second day at the shelter was much like the first. One man looked at Harley but decided he didn't bark enough and would be a poor watchdog. The man picked a scruffy looking little terrier because it barked constantly. The shelter workers realized that despite Harley's exceptional qualities, potential adopters continued to choose more needy pets.

After a week, Harley began to change. He started to become desperate for affection. He needed much more attention than he was getting from the staff. He started jumping up on the kennel door to try to nudge a passing hand. In frustration, he began barking to get attention.

One morning Harley jumped up on a kennel worker who was hosing down the kennel. The man struck Harley in the chest with his knee and sprayed him with a hose. Harley slipped and fell hard on the wet concrete. His beautiful coat was drenched with water and feces.

Harley was rapidly becoming unadoptable. Two families took him out of the kennel to look at him, but he jumped on them and smelled bad. One man decided against Harley because he barked too much. Three weeks after Harley was dropped off at the shelter, he sneezed. A little later in the day, he coughed. That night his cough got worse. Shelters don't keep sick animals. Harley was destroyed the next day.

Harley's fate is not uncommon. Well-meaning people routinely adopt animals for the wrong reasons. Humane organizations that stress the "death row" analogy unwittingly foster this tragedy.

The real reason to adopt an animal is to enhance your life. Regardless of which animal you choose, there will always be thousands more that you cannot save. Selecting an inferior animal because you feel sorry for it is a poor reason, at best. The grim fact is that there are a limited number of homes for deserving animals. The tragedy becomes ludicrous when healthy, attractive animals are destroyed while defective ones are adopted, only to be put to sleep later. If you adopt, seek the best and the brightest. Saving an animal's life may please you for the moment. Choosing the right pet will feel good for a lifetime, and you will still be saving a life.

When adopting, know what you want—and live with it

My dog, Megan, is a purebred Australian Cattle Dog. Ten years ago she was taken to an animal shelter because her behavior was completely unacceptable. She was on "death row" for the heinous offense of chasing livestock—a task that she was genetically designed to do.

In the world of domesticated animals, this scenario is not uncommon. Many pet animals are unfairly judged to be behavioral "misfits." Terriers that dig holes, Beagles that bay at the moon and cats that kill birds are good examples of animals that are condemned for displaying perfectly normal, but unacceptable, behavior.

Ironically, most of these behaviors are simultaneously prized and despised, by humans. Farm cats that stalk and hunt well are highly valued, while a city feline that performs the same behavior is a public nuisance. Beagles whose baying can be heard for miles earn praise for a hunter and a criminal citation for an urban pet owner.

Though simple ignorance is usually blamed for this paradox, the facts do not support that assumption. A person who buys an Alaskan Malamute invariably brags about the fact that they are used as sled dogs. This claim is usually left unfinished as their dog drags them briskly down the street like a sack of potatoes. Cockatiel owners often expound on their bird's verbal skills while trying to get the winged blowhard to be quiet. It is obvious that the owners are simultaneously proud and apologetic for the same behaviors.

The real culprit in this cross-species' dilemma is not ignorance, but fantasy. A major reason for picking a particular type of animal is not the reality of the animal's temperament, but the image it will project to others. Books about various breeds and species of pets pander to this process. Fighting dogs, like the Japanese Tosa, are often described as "tenacious," "powerful" and "fiercely loyal." They often attract people who want to project an image of power and control or who may be looking for unconditional love. Safari Cats, a hybrid mixture of wild and domesticated cats, are sometimes purchased because they look like little leopards.

Most often, the use of image as a means of selecting an animal backfires. The Tosa will grow to be a 200 pound animal that may casually attack the neighbor's Poodle. The Safari Cat may spray the house with urine, shred the furniture with his claws and may even attack its owner. Each animal will offer perfectly normal behavior that represents the reality behind its image.

Selecting a pet based on real, rather than imagined, qualities is the first step toward building a successful relationship. It also helps to know that for almost any beneficial trait there is an equal and opposite drawback. If you are considering acquiring a pet, these suggestions may help you decide which kind to get.

- Examine your lifestyle objectively before you decide to choose a pet. If you work 80 hours a week, even a goldfish may be too much of a responsibility. If you really want a high maintenance animal, such as a dog or horse, you should consider waiting until you can devote more time to it. If you have a new-born child you may not have the time necessary to also care for a new puppy.
- Research the type of pet you want before you buy or adopt. Do not automatically trust books or magazines about a particular breed—they are usually written by unintentionally biased enthusiasts.
- If there is a local club or organization for the type of animal that you want, see if you can attend a meeting or get to know some of the members. Seeing a perfectly trained Tasmanian Devil does not give you enough knowledge to assume that all such creatures are well behaved.
- See if you can actually borrow a similar pet from a breeder or friend. Many humane organizations and rescue clubs are looking for foster homes for pets. They may welcome an offer to have you temporarily care for a misplaced animal.

Not all dogs of a breed are alike

Glenn has owned Golden Retrievers for almost 40 years. He got his first Golden pup when he was two. He thought he knew just about everything there was to know about the breed—and then he met Sadie.

Sadie was the offspring of two field trial champions. Her grandfather was a famous hunting Retriever, and her mother's mother was both an obedience champion and a "dog show" champion. By all rights, Sadie should have been the "golden child" of the gun dog circuit. While her genes proclaimed her the beneficiary of selective breeding, her owner had a more honest assessment of her abilities. He called her a "pluperfect, golldarned, flea-infested, sorry excuse for a hair-ball. "

To get the relationship off to a good start, Sadie chewed everything in sight. Glenn could not understand it. This was like no Golden he had ever seen. Glenn really lost his temper when he found her in the middle of his workshop. She was right in the middle of his no longer water-proof waders, the shredded remains of his best shooting jacket and the shattered remnants of 150 shotgun shells. Glenn pronounced her behavior the last straw and sold her to a family that lived down the street. He vowed that he would never again own a Golden Retriever.

There is a common belief that dogs of a common breed are almost identical. We often make decisions about the type of dog to buy, based on our experiences with similar looking animals. If we have always lived with friendly German Shepherds we will assume that the next one we see will also be friendly. To carry it one step further, if we have grown up with Malamutes we may automatically like Akitas. This is not necessarily a wise leap of faith. Just because two animals look alike, they may not necessarily behave in the same way.

Scientific studies of dog genetics have yielded an interesting view of this issue. First, while puppies of a given breed may look almost exactly alike, there can be wide behavioral differences between individuals within a single litter. There can also be great differences between animals who have the same parents, but were from subsequent litters. The millions of combinations of genes possible to two individuals are not even remotely displayed within a single litter. Simply because an animal has a fine pedigree does not mean it is automatically healthy or behaviorally sound. Champion parents are perfectly capable of having "dud" offspring.

One of the difficulties with the breed system is that the criteria for breeding are often misguided. A scientific study by Drs. John Scott and John Fuller demonstrated that the genes responsible for color are not connected to behavior. Despite this finding, there are many breeders, trainers and pet owners who still believe that there are behavioral differences between black, yellow and chocolate Labrador Retrievers. Some breeders try to breed exclusively for one color and ignore potentially harmful traits— as long as the puppy is brown!

This attitude is mirrored in the way animals are judged at dog shows. Some judges develop preferences based on purely cosmetic features. While they are not supposed to, some judges invariably pick blonde Golden Retrievers over red ones, or heavier coated Norwegian Elkhounds over short coated. Ironically, other breeds, like Collies and Dachshunds, are judged separately if their coats are of dissimilar length, color or texture. This ambiguity leads to breeding animals for reasons other than health and behavioral soundness.

Another study of the differences between breeds further complicated the matter. Dr. Joe Templeton of Texas A&M University, said in a March, 1990, "Atlantic Monthly" interview, "Right now, looking at chromosomes and genetic fingerprinting, we cannot distinguish between breeds. In fact, in a comparison of two American Staffordshire Terriers with a Whippet, one Terrier appeared more closely related to the Whippet than to the other Terrier."

Using an inaccurate method for classifying breeding stock can lead to devastating side effects. The breed standards for Dalmatians calls for disqualification of dogs that have any colors other than either white with black spots, or white with liver-colored spots. If a three-colored Dalmatian was born that was absolutely free from nerve deafness (a disease common to Dalmatians) it would be eliminated from the gene pool. A dog that had the correct spot pattern might be retained even though it carried the genes for deafness. Though the physical appearance of the animal is a poor indicator of its genetic value, it is still the real underlying standard for purebreds.

If you are looking for a pet, the easiest way to select the animal is to choose it based solely on its appearance. While this is convenient, it may also lead to unexpected consequences. If you select a pet based on image, be prepared to find out the hard way—what you see is not always what you get.

Pet shop madness

"Psssst! Hey, you! Yeah, I mean you—the one reading the pet column in the Sunday newspaper! Don't look now, but you just got targeted by some real shady characters. I don't mean city thugs who strip your car. I mean sophisticated farm thugs who strip your heartstrings. You know who I mean—puppy mill breeders."

Right now, hundreds of rural families are harvesting their next winter crop of puppies. States such as Montana, Kansas, Missouri and Arkansas supply the majority of pets for sale at shopping mall pet shops. Every conceivable breed is rounded up, from Cairn Terriers to American Eskimo Dogs. They come in all sizes and shapes, but they will have several things in common: they will all look like adorable purebreds, they will be in your local pet shop by December 15th and they will be fantastically over-priced.

For these "local yokels," we "city slickers" are ripe for the picking. We are bombarded with images of puppies and kittens in automobile ads or frolicking with the kids. Our mandatory trips to the mall almost always include seeing a huge crowd pressed against the glass cages of pet shops. Invariably, some minion of Satan will comment on how lovely the Elkhound puppy is, and how it looks just like the one that he had as a child. "Oh," his fiendish voice will croon, "this one has papers! Gosh, only $900. What a bargain. I wish I hadn't maxed out my bank card!"

The words have a mysterious effect on you. Suddenly you feel as if you must possess that fantastic Elkhound, no matter what! The "man with no credit" must not be allowed to own such a wonderful dog. In sudden desperation, you muscle your way to the sales person with your trump cards—a bank card and a mall coupon worth 10% off the retail price!

"I'll take the Elkhound!" you scream to the sales person, as you fling your plastic on the counter. Within moments you are sprinting though the mall with a decidedly terrified puppy under your arm. You are trying to find your wife, blind to the fact that you are under a demonic spell. As you see the shocked look on your spouse's face, you shout, "He has papers—I got 10% off—good with kids!"

As the spell wears off, you realize that your words sound foolish. You just made the most stupid and impulsive purchase of your life. Your wife's rational reminder that you don't have any kids and her suggestion that you take the puppy back will simply make things worse. You must now tell her that you signed a paper that says you understand that the pet shop is not obligated to accept returns. The full impact of your actions finally hits you—your tobacco-spitting, country cousin has just lightened your sophisticated city wallet by several hundred dollars. You will soon find out that your precious "purebred" has a food allergy and skin problems and is terrified of guests. Three months later, your valuable purchase will be rooming at the county pound.

This slightly exaggerated scenario is not as far from the truth as you might believe. The mass production of dogs is a wide spread and lucrative business. An acre of dogs can easily produce a six-figure annual income. For people who are tired of losing crops and livestock to flood, drought and falling prices, breeding dogs is an ideal business. For an initial purchase price of a few thousand dollars, a breeder can set up a kennel with genuine purebred dogs. A wise puppy mill farmer will initially buy dogs that have impeccable pedigrees—for far less than the cost of a John Deere tractor.

Once the farmer has a few expensive purebreds, he has an open door to faking litter registrations. Since the registration of puppies is simply a matter of filling out a form, these "farmers" can easily exaggerate the number of pups in a litter. If the offspring of a cheap animal-shelter purebred are registered as the pups of a grand champion, no one is the wiser. The dog's papers are merely worthless bait meant to convince you that the price is justified.

Despite the assaults of humane groups and stricter laws, puppy mill breeders thrive. Each year they become more sophisticated at selling filthy cages full of inferior pets. The only way to stop this tragedy is for you to hang on to the only "papers" likely to be of value to you—your little yellow credit slips and pretty green dollars.

Part 6:
Problems We Cause

A nudge is as good as a nod

Mary Ann's brother, Bill, rested his hand on the arm of the couch. He had a full cup of hot coffee in his hand. Boozer, Mary's Golden Retriever, had been ignored for most of the morning and decided to do something about it. He tried bugging Mary Ann but got nowhere. Bill was visiting from Chicago and was a likely candidate to provide Boozer with some affection. Boozer approached Bill from behind and offered him his favorite behavior. He nudged Bill's elbow with his nose.

After he stopped screaming, Bill regained his composure. He rushed to the kitchen to put ice on his scalded hand and wrist. He swore at Boozer and made several outlandish statements about what he would do when he caught the dog. Boozer was so unnerved by the experience, he crawled under an end table and shook in fear.

Mary Ann rushed to the sound of her brother's scream. She hurried into the room and asked Bill what had happened. When Bill told her, she realized that Boozer's behavior had simply been an accident waiting to happen. She also realized that she had inadvertently taught the dog to spill Bill's coffee.

Many dogs display behavior that has been accidentally created and reinforced. Boozer's bumping behavior started when Mary Ann worked at her desk at home. At first, he would come and sit next to her and remain very calm. He was so endearing in his devotion that Mary Ann often dropped her hand to the top of his head and scratched behind his ears. After several seconds of rubbing and scratching, she would return to typing and forget about Boozer for a while.

Soon, Boozer would get bored and attempt to get her attention again. He would nudge her hand with the top of his nose. Within a short time, Boozer learned that if at first he didn't succeed, he should try, try again. Mary reinforced the behavior sporadically by giving Boozer an occasional pat on the head. The behavior became part of Boozer's repertoire. Whenever he wanted affection he knew how to get it—just bump someone's arm.

Teaching a behavior inadvertently is a common phenomenon. It can be something as simple as a single bark to get a chew bone, or as dangerous as attacking a stranger because the owner has unknowingly encouraged aggressive behavior. One reason for this development is that few pet owners are conscious of how affection and attention can shape and strengthen behaviors.

For instance, many pet owners attempt to "calm their dog" if it growls or lunges at other dogs or humans. The owner chants "It's OK, it's OK, be calm now," while patting and stroking the dog—an obvious positive reinforcement. The next time the dog starts to growl at another dog or person, the owner will be at a loss as to how the behavior became so strong. The dog eventually assumes that one way to get attention and affection is to growl and snap at strangers.

Another common, unintentionally reinforced behavior is jumping on people. As the dog rises from the ground on its hind legs, the typical human response is to place one's hands gently but firmly on the dog's head or forelegs and push the dog away. To the dog, this gentle nudge is a signal for more persistent jumping. Since the dog's goal is to be touched, it will continue to dance around on its hind legs as long as the human touches it.

Ending such behaviors is simple in principle but may be difficult in execution. If one simply stops reinforcing the behavior, the animal will eventually abandon it. Before the behavior is extinguished, however, the animal's initial response will be to re-double its efforts. As the dog senses that its favorite behavior is no longer working, it may attempt the behavior many times before realizing that it doesn't work anymore. To extinguish a behavior this way takes a great deal of patience but is humane and ultimately effective.

The best way to deal with behaviors such as jumping and nudging, is to be more observant of your pet's behavior. If a behavior is sometimes a nuisance to you, it will probably be unacceptable to an unsuspecting guest. One alternative is simply to allow the behavior by invitation only. Unless you ask Fido to bump you, it is not allowed. This means that he will not offer the behavior to guests or strangers, since they will be unlikely to invite him to spill their coffee. If you like having your dog jump up to greet you, you may still enjoy it without risking the behavior when your arms are full of groceries.

One of the basic features of animal behavior is its tendency to change. Learning to recognize potentially bad behaviors before they become strong is a good way to stop them. Whether you pay attention to your animal or not, what you reinforce is what you get.

Discipline is a needed part
of pet ownership

At six weeks of age, Blue was a little ball of gray fur. His fat little snout and button eyes identified him as a purebred Chow Chow. His owners, Bill and Karen, were completely infatuated with his features, and tended to be a little permissive with their new puppy's behavior. When Blue chewed up Bill's sock and got tangled in the remnants, they roared with laughter. The first time he barked and lunged at Karen to protect his rawhide toy, they were supremely amused. His antics got wilder and wilder as he grew, but neither Bill nor Karen could resist his charms.

When he was four months old, Blue started growling at their regular letter carrier. Bill thought it was the funniest thing in the world to watch Blue lunge and snap at the carrier through the heavy glass by the front door. Bill often remarked to Karen that "his little pup" was growing up and would be a fine protector someday. When Blue started growling at guests in the home, Bill shrugged it off and intuitively felt that the guests were somehow at fault.

When Blue was six months old, the Fed Ex guy stopped by with a package. As Bill opened the door to sign for the package, Blue lunged forward. The Fed Ex man needed 15 stitches in his leg, and Bill got six in his wrist from pulling the dog back inside. When Karen got home, she could not believe that her cute little pup could have done such a thing. By the time she was done talking, Bill half believed her assertion that the man must have had the smell of some other dog on him, or something. They both agreed that it had, once again, been someone else's fault.

When the animal control officer came to enforce the quarantine, Bill met her at the door. As he opened the door, he grasped Blue's collar tightly. Blue shot upward like a V-2 rocket with a defective guidance mechanism. As Bill smiled at the officer, he failed to hear or see Blue's jaws slam shut a fraction of an inch away from the officer's arm. The officer demanded that Bill put the dog outside.

"That's not necessary," explained Bill. "He's like this with everyone. He just wants to get to know you."

The animal control officer was not convinced that she wanted to get to know Blue quite that well. "Please put him outside," she said. "I need to explain the requirements of the quarantine."

Reluctantly, Bill and Karen listened about the new rules of Blue's life. For the next ten days, he would have to be on a leash any time he was not inside the house, even in the backyard. If he bit someone else during or after the quarantine period, he would automatically be ruled a vicious dog and destroyed. Bill and Karen would be legally liable for any damages he might cause, and a citation could draw a $2500.00 fine or even jail time. The officer told them it was also possible that they would be dropped from their insurance if it became known that they had a vicious dog.

When the officer left, Bill and Karen were indignant that the officer had made them put Blue outside. Anyone could see that Blue would never intentionally hurt anyone—he was just trying to get acquainted. All the talk about fines and jail were just a lot of hot air. No one was going to tell them what to do with their dog.

A few weeks later Blue nailed Bill's brother, the pool guy and a neighbor's child, all within a few days of each other. The pool guy and Bill's brother were satisfied with payment of their doctors' fees, but the kid's parents wanted "big bucks." The lawyers for Bill and Karen's insurance company explained that suits of this kind usually settled for about $80,000 above the actual costs. The kid's facial wounds would run about $40,000 or $50,000 at least.

Bill and Karen were furious that the little brat should get a dime out of them. After all, he was the one who jumped their fence to get his dumb Frisbee. Wasn't a dog supposed to attack burglars and intruders? If the kid had just stayed out of their backyard, none of this would have happened. Bill had a couple of beers and called the neighbors to tell them just where they could put their law suit.

A few weeks later, a judge ordered Blue put to sleep. Bill and Karen suffered a great deal. They couldn't understand why so many people had been "out to get them." The following Christmas, they bought another Chow Chow that they named Cinnamon. They laughed when he shredded Bill's socks and pranced around with the remnants on his head—he looked a lot like Blue.

Anthropomorphism:
A case of mistaken identity

A few days ago, I spoke with a man whose male dog was lifting his leg and urinating in the house. I asked if he had considered neutering the dog as a first step toward solving the problem. He seemed offended at the idea and told me, "No animal of mine is going to lose his manhood." He reacted exactly as if I had suggested neutering him, rather than the dog. He apparently did not understand that dogs do not have "manhood."

It is common among humans to treat an animal exactly as if it were a furry little human. This practice is called anthropomorphism. Often anthropomorphism is as harmless as talking to your pet as you would a person. For instance, we believe that Fifi "knows exactly what we are saying" because she cocks her head while she listens to us. Because the position of the dog's head looks exactly like a human pose of intense listening and concentration, we believe that she must also understand what she hears. The trouble with this practice begins when you start to base your decisions about your animal's care as if it were truly human.

Cats are often the victims of inappropriate anthropomorphic attitudes. Because humans assume that cats are aloof and uncontrollable, they are often allowed to roam and breed freely. A mother cat may be completely wild, starving and parasite ridden and still be praised for "being a good mother." Because her behavior with her kittens appears to mimic human nurturing she will gain the sympathy, but not the assistance, of her human observers. Conversely, if the animal abandons her kittens she is a "bad mother"—even though the kittens may be genetically defective.

Female dogs are not immune to anthropomorphic treatment. Many dogs are forced to have a litter of puppies in tribute to the supposed benefits of motherhood. While the general belief is that one litter will calm the dog down and make her better with kids, it is actually spaying that is more likely to cause those changes in behavior. Maternity in dogs can actually awaken undesirable behavior such as biting people in order to defend the pups.

The sex lives of dogs are also often treated as if they are identical to humans in their desires and practices. To better understand why this is inappropriate, we have to look at the process of domestication. To start with, dogs are not natural creatures. They have been systematically shaped though selective breeding for thousands of years. Not only do they not resemble humans in their sexual behavior, they no longer resemble their ancestors, the wolves.

When men first started to breed domestic dogs, they ran into a major problem. Most wolves are monogamous and usually mate for life. The first dog breeders could not simply mate any two wolves together. They had to play a Love Connection-style game of matching a suitable pair that also happened to "fall in love" with each other. So, one of the first changes caused by selective breeding was to make dogs as promiscuous as possible. If an animal was willing to mate with any other wolf it was a prime breeding animal. After ten thousand years, this behavior is retained in the rampant sexuality of the typical male dog.

So, the sex drive of dogs is not a natural phenomenon. This once necessary trait is now a major liability. When thousands of dogs are packed into relatively small areas they often react erratically because of this sexual tension. Males will jump over and dig under fences to find a female in heat. Once on the street they are in danger of automobiles, disease and the attacks of other animals. In an effort to protect the dog's libido, his owner stands a good chance of losing the animal to theft, injury and death.

In all its forms, anthropomorphism is a risky practice. Holding an animal to the same standards as a human sets them up for constant failure. Rather than attempting to force pets into a human mold, it is far more interesting to appreciate them as they are and celebrate the differences.

Dogs are not wolves—I guarantee!

A common belief among dog trainers is that much can be learned about dogs by observing wolves. For instance, wolves live in packs and dogs tend to form packs. Wolves chase and nip things and dogs tend to chase and nip things. Wolves have hair and dogs have hair. It is obvious that dogs and wolves are identical—NOT!

There is little dispute over the fact that dogs are descended from wolves. Fossil evidence indicates that dogs were domesticated about 10,000 years ago. Since that era, we have bred them into hundreds of separate breeds. Each of these breeds was developed for a purpose. Hounds chase game, while Pointers freeze and point at birds. Terriers dig underground after their quarry, while herding breeds chase cows and sheep. Few of these animals look much like wolves, but many people assume that they still behave like wolves.

A common practice among dog/wolf experts is to grab a dog by the scruff of the neck and shake it severely as a means of punishment. This is done because mother dogs supposedly shake their puppies to discipline them. Some experts promote the practice of rolling the animal on its back until it submits, in order to establish dominance. Another batch of experts suggests biting the dog's muzzle in order to establish dominance, because dominant wolves do this to exert their authority. By imitating these behaviors, according to some trainers, we can learn to communicate better with our dogs.

Before you begin a wrestling match with your dog, you may want to ask a few questions about these practices. All of these methods are assumed to be valid because they imitate the way wolves communicate with each other. This process of teaching naturally by speaking the dog's own language sounds reasonable, but what if your dog doesn't speak wolf?

The first glitch in this theory, is that it assumes that all dogs are alike, and that all of them are equally wolflike. Neither science nor casual observation confirms this assumption.

Rather than believing that all dogs are behaviorally alike, the opposite is far more believable. Kennel clubs and breeders assume that the various breeds of dogs are different from each other, and scientific research confirms this. The odds that your dog is perfectly wolflike are slim. This can lead to dramatic problems when you try to speak wolf language with your dog. While your Chow Chow may be missing the gene that tells him why you are shaking him roughly by the scruff, he may still possess the gene that tells him to bite your face.

The other common tool of wolf talkers is gripping a dog by the neck and forcing it to the ground. This is supposed to assert a leadership position over the animal. This technique is the result of inaccurate observation. Dominant wolves do not go around grabbing other wolves with their hands. They intimidate their pack mates through bared teeth, growls and bites. Even when they use a body slam to knock another animal to the ground, they do not pin them there like professional wrestlers. The secret of this relationship is that the dominant wolf does not physically hold the other animal to the ground; the subordinate wolf voluntarily submits. Unless you can create the same visual threats that a wolf can, you cannot imitate this interaction.

Another difficulty with this theory is that it flirts with the more dangerous aspects of wolf behavior. Teaching your dog that wolf-like struggles for dominance are acceptable is risky. While you may be able to control your 100-pound Akita, other guests and family members may not. If your dog is accustomed to your wolf-style dominance over him, he may think it is perfectly permissible for him to dominate lesser pack members—such as children and elderly aunts.

It is human nature to try and develop rules to explain reality. Attempts to explain dogs through their similarities to wolves are examples of this. Before you try to communicate with your dog as though he were a wolf, consider safer and more conventional methods such as positive reinforcement. If you base your training program on the belief that Rover is a wolf in dog's clothing you may be surprised—he may not understand the "call of the wild."

The school of hard knocks

Rambo, the Doberman, is chained up in the back yard. His owner is an ex-biker named Bud who hates to be bothered during dinner. Each night as Bud sits down to the table Rambo starts to bark. Bud patiently bears the noise for about 5 seconds and then storms out the back door and "thumps" Rambo. This scene is repeated several times each night until Bud's dinner is thoroughly disrupted and Rambo is thoroughly thumped. No matter how hard Bud thumps him, Rambo is prepared to bark until he gets what he wants.

Unfortunately, rather than listening to Rambo, Bud has been listening to his friend Rick. Rick knows all about dogs because his brother worked for a trainer once. Rick told Bud that if a dog gets mad at his owner it will intentionally get into trouble just for spite. Rick says that Rambo is just trying to get back at Bud for leaving him in the back yard during dinner.

To see how this apparently masochistic behavior really developed, it is necessary to ignore Rick for a moment and step outside to see the scene from Rambo's perspective.

When Rambo was about six months old he was first introduced to the chain. He hated the confinement and barked constantly for the first two days. Soon he realized that barking only worked to get him off the chain at certain times. Barking when Bud was not home was never successful in getting Rambo off the chain. He learned that if he waited until his master arrived, he had a good chance of getting free. The first few months, Bud would let Rambo off the chain after several barks. The connection between barking and freedom was firmly established in Rambo's head.

The abuse started several months later. One Friday night Bud went out for the evening. When he got home he did not immediately let Rambo off the chain. The dog barked his usual ten barks and waited for Bud to come. When ten barks failed to get him free, Rambo belted out another ten. By now, the dog realized that something was wrong. He began barking hysterically for five straight minutes. As Bud got out of the shower he heard Rambo's wild barking. That's when Rambo got his first thumping.

After a few minutes Rambo got enough courage to call his master again. Bud was feeling a little guilty over thumping Rambo. The dog let out a piteous sort of half squeak, half bark. Bud felt horrible and made a terrible mistake—he let Rambo in the house.

The next time Rambo got thumped for barking, he was no longer so timid about barking repeatedly. After his first burst of barks, he waited a few minutes and then did it again. Bud decided that he was too lenient the first time and thumped Rambo again. Bud couldn't stand to see Rambo squirming on the ground-rolling his eyes in fear. Then he made his next terrible mistake. He let Rambo in again.

Over the next few months the pattern was repeated many times. Sometimes Bud had more resolve than others and thumped Rambo persistently. Other times he responded to the first ten barks by letting the dog in. Rather than barking out of spite, Rambo was simply responding as his master taught him. He learned that if he barked long enough, and accepted several thumpings, Bud would let him inside. To Rambo, a few thumps were acceptable as long as he eventually got inside the house.

In nature, animals may often have to experience pain and discomfort to get what they want. The wolf who is kicked while attacking a caribou cannot discontinue hunting. He must be persistent, regardless of minor damage or pain. The idea that an animal will intentionally experience pain and suffering just for spite is mistaken. If a behavior persists in the face of punishment, look for the real cause of the problem—something worth "getting thumped."

Stubbornness is in the eye of the beholder

Rocky, the Boxer, goes crazy when he hears the doorbell or the faintest knock on the door. He barks and growls and leaps against the door. His owner must grab him by the collar and drag him away before a guest may enter the house. Rocky was an obedience school dropout—he was labeled "stubborn & inattentive."

A common assumption about the relative intelligence of dogs is based on their reaction to training. Dogs that adapt quickly are labeled smart while those that have difficulty are "slow." This assumption leads to an important question. If a dog does not adapt quickly to traditional training methods, could we be observing the limitations of the method more than the shortcomings of the animal?

The fastest way to test this assumption is to look at the animal's behavior objectively. Rocky's owners are convinced that he is stubborn and inattentive. They spent many hours trying to get him to respond to commands, with no luck. Yet Rocky's behavior at the door proves that he is capable of energetic and consistent performance—on his own.

If Rocky could talk, his owners would get an earful. First he would tell them that he is a dog, not a human. He has certain abilities and limitations that make it easy to learn some things and impossible to learn others. Expecting him to know right from wrong is a waste of time, but teaching him a simple association between the doorbell and strangers is easy. Next he would tell them that he really would like to cooperate, but he is not sure about what they want. Sometimes they say "Get over here," and sometimes they say "Come." They never seem to say the same thing twice. Rocky has trouble with synonyms.

When Rocky does recognize a command, it is often in the middle of some more interesting endeavor—like chasing a cat. He learned long ago that if they don't have the choke chain on him they cannot force him to ignore the cat. Pleas and offers of affection will not affect Rocky once he has become distracted. He would never pass up a chance to chase a cat in exchange for a pat on the head. He can get a pat on the head anytime. Besides, his owners have never offered anything especially pleasant for coming. In fact, they often chased him and hit him after his excursions.

This hitting is connected to several different phrases, chiefly, "You get over here, this instant!" and "Come." Rocky knows to avoid them when he hears these signals or he runs the risk of getting bopped. The more they call, the more he stays away from them.

Rocky's love for his owners eventually forces him to slink back, hours later, after he builds up his courage for the harsh words and punishment he knows will follow. Whenever Rocky does feel a need for affection he knows how to get it. When he hears the doorbell he throws himself at the door. His owner will then play tug-of-war with him and pet him to calm him down.

Each time he lunges at the stranger he gets hugged by his owner. Rocky loves the affection he gets at the front door. He listens closely for any sound that indicates that someone is coming. He knows the sequence perfectly. Rocky is really very attentive after all. He knows many commands and exactly how to respond to them. When he hears the word "come" he knows that he should run away and hide. When he hears a car door slam or footsteps approaching the house he knows the "front door game" is about to begin.

Before deciding that an animal is incapable of learning, it is valuable to look at the situation objectively. Failure to control behavior is invariably the fault of the trainer. Rocky's owner had many opportunities to see his dog's "obedience" at the front door—if he had only knocked once.

Pet the nice doggie on the head—at your own peril

Imagine a parent who tells his child to play with matches, stick his fingers in light sockets and drink liquid drain cleaner. Sounds like a serious case of child abuse, doesn't it? Yet there is another bit of equally dangerous advice that is almost universally considered acceptable: "Pat the nice doggie on the head."

There are more than 1 million reported dog bites in this country each year. There are probably four or five times that many bites that are not reported. More than 50 percent of bites involve children. It leaves some doubt as to the claim that dogs are "man's best friend."

One of the reasons for these startling statistics is the general ignorance among humans about how to properly greet a dog. The average person tries to meet a dog on purely human terms. We bend over at the waist and place our face close to the animal's. The act of patting the dog on the head is similar to the way we would greet a child. We make eye contact as a means of expressing that we are "nice." To the dog, these friendly signs of greeting are received as threats.

Each of these signals indicates to the dog that a stranger is threatening him. If you have ever watched two strange dogs meet, you will see the problem instantly. The first thing a dog does to exert his control over another dog is to make eye contact. This fixed gaze is a canine form of intimidation. While your dog might let you stare into his eyes, he is unlikely to accept the same contact from a stranger.

One part of the greeting that goes awry is touching the animal on the head, neck or shoulders. Another way that a dog displays his dominance over a subordinate is to place his neck or paw over the other animal's shoulders. Because of this, any touching or hovering over the top of the dog's head is viewed by the animal as a dominant challenge or threat of attack.

Little Billy's hug will not be perceived as a friendly gesture by Rambo, the Doberman. If a dog feels threatened or challenged, placing your hand over the dog's head or touching its neck may cost you a finger. Something as innocent as smiling may also be perceived by the dog as a threat. Dogs do show their teeth for reasons other than a warning, but not in conjunction with other threat displays. We have all seen a dog bare its teeth as a sign of warning. Showing your teeth in a friendly smile may backfire if you are also towering over the dog and making direct eye contact. Fido may interpret your movements as warning of your intent to attack.

Stiff, jerky motions are also signs of a strutting, dominant animal. When two dogs face off, they move with the mechanical gait of robots. This affected movement is another indication of the dog's malicious intent. The combination of stiff motions, eye contact and attempting to touch the dog on top of the head are instinctively perceived as signs of a supermacho dog. They also happen to be the ear marks of a staggering, uncoordinated toddler.

It is ironic that many natural and friendly behaviors of humans resemble the aggressive behaviors of dogs. Protecting children from dog bites starts with an awareness of how dogs perceive us. Avoiding the bite is often a matter of avoiding high-risk situations that could endanger the child. If you are supervising children and pets, these suggestions may be useful.

- Never allow unsupervised contact between infants and dogs. Most fatal attacks of humans by dogs involve children younger than six weeks.
- Do not allow children to approach strange dogs. If you are determined to take the risk, ask the owner's permission before the dog and child interact. Eventually the most patient dog may decide to end the mauling by returning the favor.
- Screaming and running are two behaviors that can incite predatory behavior in almost any dog. Either prevent the child from doing the behavior or confine Fido when the children are playing in this manner.

"A choke chain on one end and a 'jerk' on the other"

Sparky, the German Shepherd, was a wild and crazy dog. At ten months of age he was completely out of control. His owners, Glenn and Holly, decided to get professional help. They called a private trainer who told them he could "whip any dog into shape—in no time." He said that for several hundred dollars he would come to their house and fix the dog's problems.

Bud, the trainer, came to the house the next day. He was tall and brawny and had a military tattoo on his biceps. He quickly asked for a check and then took a choke chain and leash from his case and asked to see the dog.

Sparky's first reaction at the sight of a stranger was abrupt. He leaped up in the air and tried to lick the man's face. Bud brought his knee forward forcefully and knocked Sparky over backwards. Sparky yipped and scrambled back to his feet. He had no idea what had happened, but he knew that he must properly greet this stranger. He attempted to jump on Bud again. This time the knee hit Sparky just beneath the sternum. The dog yipped loudly and fell heavily to the ground. He scrambled up again but ducked around the corner of the house to collect his thoughts. Holly started to protest this treatment of her pet, but Bud cut her off.

"Oh, it didn't hurt him. Besides, you've got to be dominant over this dog. He's got to know who the boss is!"

Next Bud called Sparky to him and tried to loop a choke chain around the dog's head. Sparky stoutly refused to approach this two-legged demon and Glenn had to hold the dog while Bud put the chain around Sparky's neck. Sparky's eyes were wide and wild with fear.

Bud then sharply commanded "Heel!" and jerked the chain quickly and forcefully. Sparky yelped again, louder this time. Holly tried to stop the proceedings again but Bud almost teased her about being "soft" on the dog. He jerked the chain again and tugged Sparky along behind him. The severity of the first jerk had taken Sparky completely by surprise. He had never been treated like this before.

When a dog feels threatened he has four basic options—run, surrender, freeze or fight. Bud's assault had been so severe and unexpected that Sparky was forced to make a hard decision. Since he couldn't run away and he wasn't willing to simply wait to be jerked again, Sparky decided that his only option was to attack. Sparky leaped up and clamped down on Bud's arm.

Bud was caught off-guard for a split second. He had Sparky pegged as a pretty soft and cowardly type. As he noticed the blood welling up on his forearm he muttered to Glenn and Holly that now he would "have to break that habit." He continued to slash the leash and chain back and forth, preventing Sparky from either escaping or biting him.

As Bud continued his assault, Holly roused out of her shock and yelled at him to leave the dog alone and get out of her house immediately. She told him to never come back again. Rather than being upset by her attitude, Bud acted as if he were on firm ground. He said, "Lady, you signed a contract. If you don't let me come back, you still gotta pay me. So you might as well let me do the work. Besides, you got a biter on your hands—he's gotta know who's the boss."

After the trainer left, Glenn and Holly discussed their experience. As they talked, Sparky hid under the coffee table and watched them fearfully. Glenn and Holly decided that they wanted a trained dog, but this price was too great to pay. Both of them knew that Sparky had never threatened anyone before. The trainer had caused the aggression by terrifying the dog. Now he seemed to actually be afraid of them. They could not believe that this violence was necessary or beneficial.

Despite the fact that humane alternatives exist, this type of training is still common. Many people still accept the notion that pain and force somehow magically impart intelligence to an animal. If you are concerned that a training technique might be dangerous, decide before you try it on your animal. To find a trainer who can offer humane and effective methods, consult with your veterinarian, friends and local training clubs. Rather than expanding your pet's horizons, harsh training methods usually limit responses to a single goal—avoid the "jerk."

Spoiling behaviors is like spoiling food—it stinks

Vera is retired and lives in a quiet community. She has a little Pug called Tai Fun. Whenever Vera asks Tai to do anything, he completely ignores her. The only time he responds to commands is when Vera has a treat or if he thinks he is going for a walk. In case you haven't guessed, Tai is spoiled rotten.

Many pet owners lavish affection and treats on their pets as a matter of course. Regardless of performance, the dog gets plentiful food and water, verbal praise and attention. The sad truth is that a dog on this type of program is doomed to be testy, lazy and stubborn. Dogs like Tai Fun rarely pay attention to their masters because they don't have to.

In nature, predators must hunt constantly to stay alive. If a dog ignores the scents, sounds and sights of prey, he will soon die of starvation. He must be ready to react instantly to any opportunity that leads to food, water and shelter. Not surprisingly, if you take this wild animal and put him on a steady diet without the need for purposeful action he too would be as spoiled as Tai.

In fairness to Tai, his nature is not really different from a wolf in a zoo. His problem is merely that his master rewards him for being a living teddy bear. Vera uses him as a sort of security blanket. She scratches his ears and shares her popcorn with him because he "looks so cute." When her friends pet him and fuss over him, as he jumps all over their legs, they are helping to undermine any control Vera might have. When Vera finally gets tired of this behavior and attempts to tell him to sit, Tai is unlikely to respond correctly.

Vera's mistake is in assuming that because she gives her dog the best of care, that he will automatically work for her, out of loyalty and gratitude. In reality, she has taught him that when asked to perform he can afford to ignore her requests. He may occasionally have to pass up a treat for not sitting promptly, but if he waits a few minutes and looks pitiful, Vera will break down and give him something anyway.

The way to end this mess is to take some of the swagger from Tai's attitude. What he really needs is an environment that requires him to work for a living. Vera must convince him that he cannot count on a free ride anymore. She can start by getting up in the morning and making a major break with tradition— she should not automatically fill Tai's food bowl.

For Tai, this situation is unthinkable. His bowl is empty and it's past his breakfast time. He barks and whines and does everything he can think of to get Vera's attention. This is the hard part for Vera. If she gives in now, she will tell him that if he just barks loudly and long enough he can get her to do anything. Instead, Vera puts on her headphones and turns up her "Walkman." Tai is not a happy boy.

After about three minutes of yapping, Tai is absolutely frantic. He jumps on Vera's lap and gets a rude awakening—she dumps him unceremoniously on the floor. In desperation he tries his last shot at getting breakfast—he sits. As quick as a cat, Vera jumps up and fills Tai's bowl. She praises him and adds some special treats to his regular breakfast. A few more "work" sessions like this and Tai is quickly on his way to being a polite pet.

Reinforcing your pet for its mere existence is a tempting habit. Allowing a pet to become a glorified free-loader may ultimately harm your relationship. By taking pets into our homes, we must offer more than a life as "living dolls." To rephrase an old saying, " spare the job and spoil the child."

The behavioral Holy Grail—a "Magic Pill" that makes all things right

During the holidays, adults often scoff at the far-fetched wishes of children. I remember, as a child, going through the Sears catalog and outlining virtually every toy in red ink. While my parents chuckled at my outlandish desires, I was completely serious—as serious as many pet owners who dream of the "Magic Pill."

The belief in a magical pill that can solve the toughest behavior problem is all too common. I routinely speak to people who tell me that they have virtually tried everything to change their pet's behavior—to no avail. Now, just before they cart the critter to the pound, they want a miraculous solution.

For these owners, animal behavior is a malicious, spiteful and irrational thing, designed to frustrate and torment them. After months, or years of allowing a behavior to develop, they want the instant "last resort" cure—and they want it fast, cheap and guaranteed to succeed.

Foremost among these owners are the ones who have spent copious amounts of money trying to solve the problem. In search of the Magic Pill they buy electrical fences, shock collars and ultrasonic gizmos and widgets. Where an ounce of training could have stopped the problem in the first place, they assault the full blown behavior with ten pounds of cure. They are often interested in having someone take the animal away and fix it—as if it was a toaster oven or VCR.

While some owners throw money at the problem, others resolutely avoid spending one penny on training—no matter what it costs in ruined furniture or damaged landscape. One woman re-carpeted her house annually because the stench became overpowering—her dog "could not be house-trained." An alternate version of this attitude finds the owner merely adapting to the animal's inappropriate urination. A former client of mine tore up her carpet and lived on plywood for a year—she was waiting until her dog "grew out of it." Once a behavior program was finally started we found out that the dog had a physical problem that could have been cured the year before.

Even more irrational is the owner who believes that a pedigree should exempt an animal from the necessity of being trained. A common explanation is "I bought a purebred to avoid all this!"

Our culture does little to prepare us for dealing with the unacceptable behavior of animals. Good behavior, like good health, is the result of care and planning for your pet—not a Magic Pill.

- Assume that a pet's mental health requires training. Captivity does not provide the mental stimulation that an animal would get in the wild. You must train the animal yourself or have someone else do it.
- Budget training expenses into the initial cost of a pet. A timely training program can save the cost of torn curtains, chewed shoes, ruined furniture, soiled carpet and medical expenses.
- Decide if you need private or group instruction. The fees vary from $50 for a class to $500 for individual instruction. The quality of the service may have nothing to do with the price. Ask your veterinarian for a recommendation.

If you are irritated by your pet's behavior, consult your veterinarian first—immediately! Some behaviors are caused by medical problems. You risk your pet's health by taking the advice of well-meaning friends, relatives and breeders. If the problem is not physical, your veterinarian may suggest a qualified behaviorist.

Second pet may be "double trouble"

Bubba, the Bull Terrier, was devoted to his family. He loved to be with them and feared being left alone. Whenever the family would leave, Bubba would become so anxious that he would destroy anything he could sink his teeth into. The family decided to fix Bubba's problem by getting him a companion.

Bubba's first introduction to his new companion was on a Saturday. The family returned from their trip to the pound with Bubba's new playmate, Rex. They placed the cute little Retriever on the ground and expected to see Bubba wag his tail in appreciation. Bubba was not amused. The new puppy had no manners at all. He jumped on Bubba and bit his ears. Rex tried to steal Bubba's food and got nipped for his trouble. Worst of all, the new puppy was the center of attention. The family spent half of their time telling Bubba that he should appreciate his new brother and half the time fussing with the little nuisance. Bubba tried to stay as far away from the thing as possible.

Staying away from the puppy was impossible. The family shut them both in the laundry room when they left the house. Bubba still panicked when his owners left home. The puppy watched Bubba violently attacking the clothes basket and joined in. When the family got home they assumed that Bubba had made the entire mess and whacked him with a newspaper.

This pattern soon became the routine for Bubba and Rex. The family would put them together whenever they left the house. Soon Bubba became accustomed to the comings and goings of the family. He actually stopped his frantic destruction. He would simply lie huddled in a corner, away from "Rex the Hex."

Hex was a good term for Rex's relationship to Bubba. While Bubba had become nondestructive, Rex had taken over the behavior, out of boredom. Each day the family would return home and discover another item destroyed in the laundry room. They would dutifully punish Bubba for his supposed transgression. Each day Rex would find another thing to destroy. Each day Bubba got the spanking.

This undeserved beating started to make Bubba unstable. He couldn't understand why his owners attacked him every time they came home. Now Bubba had to be dragged into the laundry room. He thought of it as an evil place. One day as the father dragged Bubba to the laundry room, the dog bit him on the wrist. Bubba didn't want to bite his owner, but he was terrified. He simply could not bear another day in the evil laundry room. He scampered behind the couch and cringed in fear. The father ran to the couch and pulled it away from the wall. A very frightened Bubba tried to dive farther away from this bellowing maniac. The father grabbed Bubba by the collar and dragged him toward the laundry room.

Bubba felt the hand on his neck and tried to resist. The thickness of his own neck made it impossible to bite the man again. He was tossed roughly into the laundry room for the last time. Bubba was taken to the pound the next day. The man said that he refused to own any animal that would dare to bite him. He told the people at the pound that Bubba couldn't be trusted— he had turned on his owner.

Several days later the family realized that Rex was destructive too. They called a trainer to work on the problem. Rex was a good dog that was worth fixing. Besides, they thought, it must have been Bubba's fault that Rex tore things up. They also considered getting a second dog to keep Rex company.

Acquiring a playmate for an animal is often used as a cure-all for poor behavior. If the pet's behavior is the result of bad training, the owner is probably going to create a second little monster to mirror the first. Before deciding to get a second animal, consider the possible benefits and drawbacks of your decision. While companionship may be the missing ingredient in your dog's mental health, it is your companionship that is most likely to do the trick.

Inadvertent reinforcement

Buddy is a four-month-old Fox Terrier puppy that loves to chew and nip at the hands of his owner, Mark. After reading a book on training, Mark tried to stop the biting behavior by distracting Buddy with a rawhide toy whenever the biting occurred. The book said to shout the word "NO!" at the dog. Then, when the biting stopped, praise the dog and give him something else to chew on.

The first few times Mark tried this method, Buddy just about jumped out of his skin when he heard the word "NO!." The biting behavior decreased because he was too busy with the rawhide to bite anyone. Then something odd happened—Buddy started nipping more often and started biting harder. Soon he stopped reacting to the word "NO!." When Mark tried to distract Buddy with the rawhide, the dog would only chew on it for a few seconds, and then return to chewing on Mark. Mark was unsure what to do, so Buddy helped out as much as he could by chewing up the training book.

Ideally, teaching and learning should be connected. All too often, what we intend to teach is not what the animal actually learns. Buddy is a good example of a common problem—mixing reinforcements. Reinforcements are things that strengthen behaviors. Positive reinforcers are things that we will actively work to get, like food, shelter and flowers. Negative reinforcers are things that we work to avoid, such as pain, fruit cake and tight shoes. Mark's problem was that he mixed the two together. Without knowing it, he strengthened the very behavior he was trying to eliminate.

Buddy's reaction to the reinforcements was typical. At first he was repelled when Mark said "No!" As Buddy cringed and backed off, Mark shoved a rawhide bone at him and praised him. He didn't like the yelling, but he sure did like the rawhide. The next time he wanted a rawhide bone he tried his new behavior. First, he bit Mark on the hand and braced himself for the shout that was to follow. Mark obliged him by shouting loudly and then giving him a rawhide bone. Buddy was thrilled! It worked!

The way to avoid this situation is very simple. Make each repetition of the behavior a distinct experience for the dog. Mark should have said "NO" and then scooted Buddy from the couch, or removed him from the room. After a few minutes Mark should have asked Buddy back on the couch for a fresh chance. On this new repetition, Buddy can receive either positive reinforcement or punishment, depending on his behavior. If he doesn't bite, he can receive the affection that he craves. If he nips, he is punished by being ignored for a few minutes.

Once Mark resolves the biting problem, he will have the key to another of Buddy's behaviors. Whenever Mark is on the phone, Buddy barks at him. At first Mark thought Buddy was crazy. Mark certainly didn't teach the dog to bark at him—or did he? Mark remembered that when the behavior first started he tried to stop the behavior using the same technique he used to stop the nipping. He shouted "No," and as soon as Buddy stopped, he picked Buddy up and cuddled him. Without realizing it, Mark had reinforced Buddy's barking many times by picking him up. When Mark failed to pick him up, Buddy would bark louder. Soon the behavior was out of control.

The key to good training is picking the proper reinforcements and applying them in the right order, with good timing. If a chain of behaviors includes punishment but ends in positive reinforcement, it may become strengthened, regardless of your intent.

Learn more about
Positive Reinforcement Training

PRODUCTS

By

Gary Wilkes

Visit Our Web Site At:
http://www.clickandtreat.com

For more information
call 1-602-649-9804

for a free catalog
call 1-800-456-9526

or write
CLICK & TREAT™ PRODUCTS
2344 E. Alpine Ave.
Mesa, Arizona 85204